ersity
an

Anthony Trollope

BARCHESTER TOWERS

Notes by Ian Milligan
MA M ED (GLASGOW)
Lecturer in English, University of Stirling

LONGMAN
YORK PRESS

YORK PRESS
Immeuble Esseily, Place Riad Solh, Beirut.

LONGMAN GROUP LIMITED
Longman House,
Burnt Mill,
Harlow,
Essex

First published 1986
ISBN 0 582 79265 7
Produced by Longman Group (FE) Ltd
Printed in Hong Kong

Contents

Part 1: Introduction *page* 5
The life of Anthony Trollope 5
Barchester Towers and the Church of England 7
A note on the text 12

Part 2: Summaries 13
A general summary 13
Detailed summaries 15

Part 3: Commentary 61
Studying the novel 61
The design of *Barchester Towers* 63
The structure of the novel in detail 66

Part 4: Hints for study 90
Some specimen questions 104
Two specimen answers 105

Part 5: Suggestions for further reading 107

The author of these notes 109

Part 1
Introduction

The life of Anthony Trollope

Anthony Trollope was born in 1815. His father was a barrister whose hopes of inheriting his uncle's estate were dashed when that elderly gentleman married a young wife. His mother, Frances Trollope, was a lively, sociable woman of great intelligence. Early in his career, Trollope's father's ambitions began to suffer from his rigid and opinionated character. He leased a farm near Harrow and built a large house there. For a time things went well, but gradually his financial position became more precarious. Trollope, as the youngest son of the family, suffered more from these financial reverses than his brothers. He was first sent as a day-boy to Harrow school; when he was twelve, he went to Winchester, his father's old school. While he was there, his mother took the other children to America in an attempt to repair the family fortunes. In 1830 he returned to Harrow school, walking the three miles from his home to school four times a day. He was not regarded as a clever or attractive boy; indeed, he was despised for his dullness and poverty.

The family fortunes were not improved by Mrs Trollope's commercial activity in America, but the book she wrote about her experience, *Domestic Manners of the Americans* (1832) was an immediate success. At the age of fifty-two, forced by necessity to be the bread-winner of the family, Mrs Trollope began a career as a best-selling novelist. She moved the family to Belgium, where almost immediately two of her children fell ill of consumption. Anthony returned to London in 1834 to take up a clerkship in the London Post Office. He was awkward, shy and unused to being alone in a city. In his *Autobiography*, published in 1883, a year after his death, he says:

> I wonder how many young men fall utterly to pieces from being turned loose into London after the same fashion? Mine was I think of all phases of such life the most dangerous. When I reached London no mode of life was prepared for me – no advice even given to me. I went into lodgings and then had to dispose of my time . . . It seems to me that in such circumstances the temptations of loose life will almost certainly prevail with a young man.

Some of the temptations are recorded in his descriptions of the young clerks and public servants who appear in his novels. Trollope survived them for seven years, no doubt seeing much in London that he could put to good use in his later novels.

In 1841, after a serious illness, he applied for a clerkship in the Surveyor's office (a branch of the Post Office) in the West of Ireland. There he learned to enjoy hunting, became engaged and was married, and wrote his first novel: by slow degrees and patient effort he had made for himself a place in the community. But his first attempts at writing brought him little success. It was not until he returned to England in 1851 on Post Office business that he found his true subject-matter in the social complexities of English life. His first English novel, *The Warden*, based on a contemporary scandal about the wrongful use of charitable funds, was begun in 1851 and published in 1855. Its modest success led him to write *Barchester Towers* (1857). Official business involved Trollope in much travelling – in Egypt, Scotland, and the West Indies. In 1859 he was transferred from Ireland to the eastern part of England, where he settled down to a life of energetic pleasures, the comfort of family life and his twin occupations as novelist and Post Office official. His first great popular success was with *Framley Parsonage* (1861), which was serialised in the new *Cornhill Magazine*, edited by W.M. Thackeray (1811-1863). By 1864 he had completed five of the six novels set in Barsetshire, and begun the series of political novels (the Palliser novels) which refer frequently to English parliamentary life. He was associated with many of the influential periodicals of the time, such as *The Pall Mall Gazette* and the *The Fortnightly Review*, but his own attempt at editing such a periodical – *St Paul's Magazine* – was not a success. This relative commercial failure, and his failure to win a seat in Parliament in 1868, coincided with the beginning of his decline as a popular novelist. Between 1860 and 1870 he had written more than twenty novels, as well as stories, books of travel and a political biography. In 1873, after a visit to his son in Australia, he began *The Way We Live Now* (1875), a critical and satirical novel about contemporary English society whch many consider to be his finest novel. He continued to write prolifically until his death in 1882, finding time to write even on his travels on the Continent, to Australia, to South Africa and to Iceland. In the last year of his life he made two journeys to Ireland to collect material for a novel, called *The Landleaguers*, set in Ireland, on which he was working when he died. His *Autobiography*, written in 1876 but not published until 1883, damaged his reputation because of its detailed description of the disciplined effort which had gone into his work. Trollope presented himself as a dedicated craftsman who was keenly interested in the commercial success of his novels. That book, however, has become recognised as one of the most enjoyable nineteenth-century autobiographies. Trollope's quality of humane common sense and his insight into human motivation have long since rescued him from the mild contempt in which he was held by a later generation which prided itself on a more sophisticated taste.

Barchester Towers and the Church of England

Readers of *Barchester Towers* must begin by understanding the dominant part which religion and religious ideas played in English social life up to the middle of the nineteenth century – and, indeed, beyond. The idea of God and of his governance over all human affairs was held unquestioningly by the great majority. There was an intimate relationship between the Church of England and the State: people found it easy to believe that the well-being of the nation was closely connected with the religious beliefs and moral practices the Church taught to its members. The spiritual territory of the Church was co-extensive with the boundaries of the nation.

This state of affairs had not come about without considerable struggle within the nation. The Church of England had been established in 1534 by King Henry VIII as the state religion with the king as 'the only supreme head on earth'. Between 1534 and 1689 there had been many disputes about the character of the Church of England, but it had not been generally disputed that there should be a national church. By the end of the seventeenth century these disputes had caused more social disruption than most people were willing to endure. There followed a long period of quiet acceptance that the Church was the religious and ideological arm of the State.

Much of the history of the nineteenth century was to reveal that this reconciliation was temporary. The old animosities between the Catholic and Protestant (the high church and low church) wings of the Church of England had not completely disappeared. Some churchmen were willing to question the domination of the spiritual authority of the Church by a State which was becoming increasingly secular, less convinced that what the Church taught was true, less interested in the idea of the active participation in the affairs of the world by a supreme Deity. It appeared that the claim of the Church to represent the whole of the nation was less plausible. The price of the harmony which had been gained at the end of the seventeenth century had been the exclusion of many ministers and believers who did not accept the middle way between Roman Catholicism and Calvinism, which the theologians of the Church of England had formulated and developed. These Dissenters, as they were called, joined the Roman Catholics in a state of permanent exclusion from the Church of England and from many of the purely secular privileges, such as access to University education, which were reserved for members of the national church. The membership of these churches had grown and immigrants from Ireland had increased the number of Roman Catholics in England. The Church of England had been established in the old centres of population: its organisation found it difficult to adapt to the changing patterns of a society which was becoming industrialised.

Barchester Towers does not deal with all these problems, but many of them are referred to in the course of the novel and Trollope takes it for granted that the reader understands the structure of the Church and the controversies which had been renewed by the realisation by successive governments that the settlement of the relationship between the Church and the State which had been arrived at by the end of the seventeenth century was no longer satisfactory. Dissenters and Roman Catholics were significant constituencies within the state: they must be allowed to have the full rights of a citizen of the country. Many members of the Church of England saw an increase in the freedom of those who were not members of the Church of England as an attack on the privileges of the Church. The Church, some argued, was in danger from its state partner: perhaps, it should strengthen itself by separating from the influence of the State and by conducting a process of purification which would clarify the beliefs of the Church, and impose on all church members a re-defined set of beliefs and practices. Trollope's interest as a novelist lies in the dramatic possibilities he saw in the tension which these renewed arguments produced. Characters such as Bishop Proudie, Mrs Proudie and Mr Slope, Archdeacon Grantly and Mr Arabin represent the positions of some of these internal disputes within the Church. Important as they were, of course, they represented only one strand of the fabric of social life. There are many people in ordinary life who are not primarily interested in such matters even though they may be affected by them. Clergymen are attracted by members of the opposite sex and wish to marry them. They are ambitious for worldly success and may try to use their beliefs to gain it, or may have to adapt to keep the favour of powerful people who do not share them. It is the interaction of these manifold and conflicting interests and aims which Trollope has taken as his subject in *Barchester Towers*.

The constitution of the Church of England

The Church of England was (and is) an elaborate hierarchical institution, which had very great authority over the lives of the people of the country. From early times spiritual and temporal affairs were closely linked. Churches were built on land which had an owner and was subject to the laws relating to the holding of land; they were only temporarily entrusted to the minister and church officials who looked after them. The development of the organisation of the Church was a slow growth incorporating many diverse and sometimes apparently conflicting interests. Although *Barchester Towers* can be read and enjoyed without a close knowledge of these matters in detail, readers who know something of the nature of the constitution of the Church will be more aware of the richness and subtlety of the novel.

Since the beginning of the ninth century AD the Church in England has been divided into two provinces governed by the archbishops of York and Canterbury respectively. There were twenty-six dioceses, or areas of the country under the spiritual guidance of a bishop, in England and Wales. All the bishops, including, of course, the archbishops of York and Canterbury, had seats in the House of Lords; later, as their number grew, the number of seats was kept the same and bishops were appointed to their seats in the House of Lords on the basis of seniority. The bishops, therefore, had a part to play in the national life, and in politics, as well as in the spiritual lives of those who lived within their dioceses. To help in his spiritual work (his 'cure of souls'), the bishop was originally assisted by a deacon who acted as his secretary and companion. As the number of these assistants grew, they in turn were supervised by an archdeacon who gradually assumed rights which had once been held only by the authority of the bishop. Thus the archdeacon had a measure of independent power within the bishopric. He would have a district for whose clergymen he was responsible and over whom he had powers of inspection and discipline.

From the time of their establishment the bishops attracted to them other clergymen who lived in community with the bishop at his cathedral, the principal church in the region under his control, in which was established his throne ('cathedra') and from which he governed his diocese (or 'bishopric', or 'see'). The clergy of the cathedral (the canons) formed a corporation called the chapter, at the head of which was the dean.

Originally, the bishops and their assistants performed the services of worship themselves by visiting their episcopal districts from their cathedrals. But gradually fixed places for the celebration of worship by individual priests were established; land was given on which churches could be built; and districts (or parishes) were established within which the priests could officiate. The parish church was able to raise income from compulsory payments (tithes) which were made by the parishioners from their earnings or from the produce of their lands. Sometimes the priest was responsible independently for the management of this property and income, in which case he was called 'rector', and was able to apply a proportion of the income to his own use. Sometimes the management of the parish was in the hands of a cathedral or other body, which had the right to appoint a vicar at a salary determined by the governing body. But the rectors or vicars did not have to be resident in the parish. One man might hold a number of livings, or benefices, and assistants, called 'curates', could be appointed at a much lower salary to act as a substitute for the holder of the living. Clergymen who had been appointed to a number of livings were often called 'pluralists' and they were frequently the cause of considerable concern.

The Church in the nineteenth century

Political reform in England was long delayed by the fears that had been aroused by the French Revolution. A period of repressive government after the Napoleonic wars had given way to a more relaxed climate of opinion in which an increase in the numbers of those thought fit to participate in the electoral system of the country could be contemplated. In 1832, after much delay and hesitation, the first Reform Bill passed through its stages in Parliament. The Church of England in the nineteenth century seemed to need as much administrative reform as Parliament itself. In fact the first major step towards the reform of the organisation of the church was taken by Sir Robert Peel, a Conservative Prime Minister, who set up in 1835 a body which became known as the Ecclesiastical Commission. The task of this body was to redistribute the income of the Church so that the worst inequalities of income among its clergy might be removed. A number of Acts of Parliament continued this work of reform. Bishops were not allowed to hold livings in conjunction with their sees; their salaries (stipends) were equalised; new sees were established to take account of the growth of population in the manufacturing areas of the North of England. The number of benefices held by one clergyman was limited to two, not more than ten miles apart; services were to be held more regularly and the clergyman was to be required to live in his parish. The Dean and Chapter Act of 1840 reduced the number of resident canons to four, though bishops were allowed to appoint unpaid canons to the cathedral as a mark of their distinction as clergymen. Deans were to be appointed by the government. This work of reform took time: non-resident canons and holders of pluralities were not deprived immediately of their benefices. When the current holder died, the new conditions came into force. So it came about that in *Barchester Towers*, a novel set in the middle fifties, Dr Vesey Stanhope is an absentee clergyman, who lives in Italy with his family on the income he derives from his prebend as a canon of the Cathedral and from 'the two large rectories of Crabtree Canonicorum and Stogpingum'.

Evangelicals, Tractarians and 'High and Dry' Churchmen

Central to the structure of *Barchester Towers* is the idea of conflict within the Church of England. Three clergymen in particular represent different strands of the church tradition. Mr Slope, the Bishop's chaplain, stands for the enthusiastic, missionary wing of the church – the Evangelicals; Mr Arabin represents a new force, stemming from the Tractarians, which stressed the link the Church of England had with its Catholic tradition, and Archdeacon Grantly, imperious, wealthy and a little worldly, is a clergyman of the old 'high and dry' school which valued the link between the Church of England and the State and considered the clergyman to be a close ally of the squire.

It may be thought that Trollope's portrait of Mr Slope, and of his patron Mrs Proudie, is scarcely fair to those members of the Church of England who, since the middle years of the eighteenth century, had tried to improve and intensify the quality of religious life. When Trollope was writing *Barchester Towers* the Evangelical party in the Church of England seemed to have gained an advantage, since the leading Evangelical layman, Lord Shaftesbury (1801-1885), was the son-in-law of the Prime Minister's second wife. Many ecclesiastical appointments made by Lord Palmerston (1784-1865) were thought to have been influenced by his advice. The activities of the Society for Promoting Due Observance of the Lord's Day, founded in 1831, had annoyed many people since it had attempted to stop the running of trains on Sunday and the opening of shops. The British Museum and the National Gallery were not allowed to open on Sundays, the Great Exhibition of 1851 was closed on Sunday and bands were forbidden to play in the parks. Lord Shaftesbury believed that the laws of the state should be in conformity with the law of God and it might have appeared to some people, including Trollope, that the Evangelicals in the Church of England were in danger of establishing such an influence in the state that their conception of how life should be lived might be imposed on everyone. Of course, the aim of Trollope's satire of Mr Slope and Mrs Proudie is narrower and more personal than these observations might suggest. It is the discrepancy between what his characters say and what they do which principally interests Trollope: behind the most fervent professions of Christian devotion lie more squalid appetites for power, self-aggrandisement and (in Mr Slope's case, at any rate) sexual gratification.

Another group of clergymen had formed a party in nineteenth-century England. Known as 'Tractarians' or 'Puseyites', because one of their leaders was Dr Edward Pusey (1800-82), they had caused much discussion by issuing a series of pamphlets called *Tracts for the Times* which challenged assumptions about the relationship between Church and State, and tried to assert the Catholic belief in the traditions of the Church, as opposed to the Protestant belief in the primacy of the individual believer's experience of God through prayer and the reading of the Bible. The principal spokesman of this group was John Henry Newman (1801-92) who became a member of the Roman Catholic Church in 1845. This group of theologians was associated with the University of Oxford (and was also known as the Oxford Movement) but the implications of their views were thought to be divisive and led many to wonder whether it was still possible to support the Church of England, which in the view of the Tractarians had become too subservient to the control of the State. In *Barchester Towers* Mr Arabin is the representative of this way of thinking. Trollope presents him as a man who had supported the Tractarians until it became clear that their path led to Rome. He had then undergone a conversion which restored his belief in the necessity of personal piety and led him to a reaffirmation of the relationship between the individual worshipper and his God. Thus he was led back to an acceptance of the broad tolerant faith of the Church of England and was welcomed back by his College as a Fellow.

Dr Grantly, the Archdeacon of Barchester, represents the more worldly side of the Church of England. He is strongly attached to the Church as an established institution. He is aware of its social prestige and is emotionally, rather than intellectually, convinced of the value of its traditions. Dr Grantly thinks more of power than of piety. As archdeacon he has his own territory and responsibilities. He is not disposed to accept the authority of the new bishop uncritically and is as much aware of the political divisions which separate them as of the Christian beliefs which ought to bring them together. 'High and dry' clergymen, such as he, were mainly concerned to defend the settlement between Church and State which had been arrived at in 1689, after the expulsion of James II (1633-1701) who had tried to make Roman Catholicism the official religion of the country. Their loyalty was to Church and King rather than to Parliament which they did not expect to interfere in Church affairs.

A note on the text

The first edition of *Barchester Towers* was published by Longman in three volumes in 1857. Later reprints in Trollope's lifetime were published in one volume. The manuscript has not survived. Trollope's correspondence about the novel with Longman may be found in Michael Sadleir's *Trollope: a Commentary*, with notes by R. W. Chapman, Constable, London, 1927, pp.160-6.

Part 2

Summaries
of BARCHESTER TOWERS

A general summary

The novel opens as the Bishop of Barchester lies on his death-bed. His son, Archdeacon Grantly, hopes to succeed him but before he can do so there is a change of government. Dr Grantly is a Tory high churchman; the new government prefers to appoint liberal-minded Whigs. The new bishop, Dr Proudie, and his domineering wife arrive in Barchester with their chaplain, Mr Slope. They are earnest Evangelicals; Mrs Proudie and Mr Slope aim to bring about reforms in Barchester. One appointment which is vacant is the wardenship of Hiram's Hospital, a charitable foundation, which had been held by Mr Harding, an old friend of the former bishop and the father-in-law of Dr Grantly. His younger daughter, Eleanor, is the widow of John Bold, whose zeal for reform brought about Mr Harding's resignation from the post. Now the charity has been reconstituted, and Mr Harding hopes he may be reappointed to the position he loved. Bishop Proudie is perfectly willing that Mr Harding should have the wardenship, but he leaves the detailed arrangements to Mr Slope who suggests conditions which Mr Harding is unwilling to accept. Mr Slope then turns to another clergyman, Mr Quiverful, whose large family makes him more willing to do what he is told. Mr Slope, however, then discovers that Eleanor Bold, Mr Harding's daughter, is wealthy and marriageable. He tries to retract his offer of the wardenship to Mr Quiverful and supports Mr Harding's claim.

Mrs Proudie, the Bishop's wife, is not pleased at his change of mind. She has already been upset by Mr Slope's conduct at a party she had given for the notables of Barchester at which he had shown too great an interest in Signora Neroni, the daughter of a Barchester clergyman who had long resided in Italy. She is still married to an Italian from whom she had separated. Her father, Dr Stanhope, had recently returned to Barchester with his impecunious and unconventional family. Mrs Proudie is determined to show Mr Slope that she is the most influential member of the bishop's household. But the bishop supports Mr Slope and it appears that Mr Quiverful will not become warden. Since Mr Slope has incurred the wrath of the Barchester clergy by appearing to instruct them in their duties, Dr Grantly is glad to welcome as vicar of St Ewold's, Mr Arabin, an Oxford scholar, who has long been an opponent of Mr Slope's doctrinal views. Eleanor Bold makes friends with the Stanhopes and the Stanhope sisters think her a suitable match for their feckless brother Bertie, who has incurred many debts. Dr Grantly, however, invites Eleanor to visit him and his wife at the rectory at Plumstead to meet Mr Arabin and the local landowners, Mr and Miss Ullathorne, who are the patrons of St Ewold's. Meanwhile, Mr Slope attempts to persuade Mr Quiverful to renounce his hopes of the wardenship in favour of Mr Harding. Mrs Quiverful goes to Mrs Proudie whose attempts to intervene are thwarted by Mr Slope. His letter to Eleanor Bold informing her of the new turn of events causes much disharmony at Plumstead. Dr Grantly recognises the chaplain's handwriting and suspects that an undesirable friendship has sprung up between Eleanor and Mr Slope. Eleanor refuses to divulge the contents of the letter and is shocked to learn that Mr Arabin appears to believe she may consider marrying Mr Slope. Although Mr Arabin begins to suspect he has made a mistake, there is a rupture in their relationship and Eleanor leaves Plumstead angry at the misperceptions of her friends. In Barchester, Signora Neroni exposes the insincerity of Mr Slope's attachment to herself, making clear her knowledge of his interest in Mrs Bold.

The sudden illness of the aged Dean of Barchester raises the question of who will succeed him. Mr Slope has no doubt of his own claims to the post and seeks the assistance of the bishop and other influential friends. Mrs Proudie ridicules the idea and shows that she intends to bring about Mr Slope's departure from Barchester. In Oxford it is suggested that Mr Harding might become the new dean. The complex plot of the novel takes clearer shape during the fête held by Miss Thorne at Ullathorne. Against a background of revived medieval sports and the jostling for attention of persons of all the classes of Barsetshire, Eleanor Bold is proposed to, first, by Mr Slope whose face she slaps, and then, half-heartedly, by Bertie Stanhope. She rejects them both and returns to Barchester. While the fête is in progress the death is announced of the Dean of Barchester. The bishop confirms the appointment of Mr Quiverful as warden of the Hospital. The signora takes a hand in Eleanor's love-affairs by telling her how much Mr Arabin loves her. She publicly humiliates Mr Slope by sneering at his hopes of preferment and of romance and exposes the deceitfulness he has practised in pursuit of them. To everyone's surprise Mr Harding is offered the vacant deanery. Miss Thorne takes a hand in match-making by bringing Eleanor and Mr Arabin together at Ullathorne. An engagement between them is quickly concluded, to the astonishment of Dr Grantly and the delight of Mr Harding who has the idea that Mr Arabin should become dean. A word in the right places soon brings about his appointment. Mr Slope returns to London after bitter words with Mrs Proudie. The Stanhopes go back to Italy, and the cathedral of Barchester is left in the safe hands of the High Church Party who have successfully thwarted the unwelcome innovations of a low-church bishop and his interfering wife.

Detailed summaries

Chapter 1: Who will be the New Bishop?

Dr Grantly, the old bishop of Barchester, lay dying. His son, Archdeacon Grantly, had been given a hint that he might be appointed on his father's death by the government of the day. But on the day his father died, news came that the government had fallen. A telegram intimating that the bishop was dead, sent to the Prime Minister by the bishop's old friend, Mr Harding, who was the archdeacon's father-in-law, was passed on to his successor, who was not bound by the intention of his predecessor. After some delay, and much speculation in the press, it was announced that Dr Proudie was to be the new Bishop of Barchester.

NOTES AND GLOSSARY:

as the ministry of Lord– was to give place to that of Lord– : Lord Derby (1799-1869) left office in December 1852, but the incoming Whig administration referred to is that of Lord Palmerston who took office in February 1855

proverb with reference to the killing of cats: 'There are more ways of killing a cat than choking it with cream'

the Master of Lazarus: Lazarus is the beggar in the New Testament parable (Luke 16: 19-25). Trollope is making a joke about the current wealth of colleges often founded as charities for poor scholars

telegraph message: the Morse electric telegraph was first used publicly in 1844

sea-coal fire: coal which was obtained from seams exposed by the sea. It is often praised for its warmth and wholesomeness

a Newmarket list: a list of the horses which were at Newmarket, a racing centre in West Suffolk, established since the seventeenth century

***The British Grandmother . . . The Anglican Devotee . . . The Eastern Hemisphere*:** Trollope's fictitious names for some of the rival sectarian papers of the time

***The Jupiter*:** Trollope's name for *The Times*, founded 1785, which was often known as 'The Thunderer'

***nolo episcopari*:** (*Latin*) 'I do not want to be a bishop'. This is the traditional reply to the offer of a bishopric. Trollope believes it to be rather insincere

Dickens: Charles Dickens (1812-70), English novelist, whose *Little Dorrit* appeared in monthly numbers from December 1855 to June 1857

Fitzjeames: a reference to W.M. Thackeray, the English novelist, one of whose comic characters was a footman who had risen in the world and who supposedly contributed articles to *Punch* under the name Fitzjames de la Pluche

Sydney Smith: (1771-1845), English clergyman, writer and wit, associated with the *Edinburgh Review* (founded 1802)

'last infirmity of noble minds': see *Lycidas*, line 71, by John Milton (1608-74)

Ecclesiastical Commission: a body, originally established by Sir Robert Peel (1788-1850) in 1835, into whose hands was given the administration of the revenues of the Church of England. It began a process of reforming the inequalities in the stipends (salaries) paid to clergymen

to sit in full lawn sleeves among the peers of the realm: twenty-six bishops were allowed to have seats in the House of Lords

Chapter 2: Hiram's Hospital according to Act of Parliament

Mr Harding had been warden of a charitable institution for poor old men, endowed under the will of John Hiram, until a zealous reformer, John Bold, had accused him of enjoying the income which ought properly to have gone to the old men who lived in Hiram's Hospital. Stung by this attack, Mr Harding had resigned his wardenship and settled down modestly as rector of one of the Barchester churches and director of music of the Cathedral. His behaviour had been widely praised, but he did not try to gain any further promotion. The position of warden at the hospital remained unfulfilled and the affair was forgotten. After some years a bill was introduced into Parliament to establish the Hospital on new principles: women as well as men were to enjoy the charity of John Hiram, and a matron and a steward were to be appointed under the guidance of a warden. Dr Proudie, the new bishop, was to be responsible for these appointments.

Although John Bold's reforming zeal had harmed the interests of Mr Harding, he had wooed and married Mr Harding's daughter, Eleanor, leaving her soon afterwards a widow with a young son, who was adored by his mother, his mother's sister, who was the wife of Archdeacon Grantly, and by his father's sister, Mary Bold. Eleanor thought of her husband with deep affection. He had left her well provided for: she intended to look after her fortune for the benefit of her son.

NOTES AND GLOSSARY:

the precentor of the cathedral: a member of the clergy of a cathedral who leads or directs the singing

the primate: the archbishop

the Royal Chapel at St James's: the chapel at the Royal Court of St James at Westminster

the *Musical Scrutator*: an imaginary musical review

Cassandra: the daughter of Priam, King of Troy, who had the gift of prophecy but who was never believed

the Upper House: the House of Lords

radical member: one of the followers of the English jurist, Jeremy Bentham (1748-1832), who believed in the reform of institutions on rational lines

the first threatenings of a huge war: the Crimean War began in March 1854

its eleven stages: each of the two Houses in Parliament gives each bill a First and Second reading, a committee stage, a report stage and a Third reading. The bill then is given the Royal Assent

Chapter 3: Dr and Mrs Proudie

Dr Proudie had been a clergyman in London whose duties had brought him to the attention of powerful political patrons. He was connected by birth to the nobility and his views were fashionably liberal. Although he had no great originality or intelligence, he was tactful, well-mannered and dignified. He believed he deserved to be promoted and had ambitions beyond Barchester. The bishop's wife was a woman of determined character. She was conscious of her own social position and ruled her house and her husband with a rod of iron. Since in her eyes he could do nothing right, the bishop had become accustomed to submitting to her judgement not only in domestic affairs but in the business of the diocese. The bishop's daughters had no high opinion of their father and were not specially devout young women. Mrs Proudie adamantly believed in the strict observance of Sunday as a day devoted to religious duties. In these views she was supported by Mr Slope who had given up his post in London to attend the Bishop as his domestic chaplain.

NOTES AND GLOSSARY:

Ecclesiastical courts: courts for administration of church law and maintaining the discipline of the Established Church of England

chaplain . . . almoner: in this context these terms are synonymous. They refer to the ceremonial duties of a clergyman in a royal household. Queen Victoria had many German cousins. The references in this section may have their origin in the career of Bishop Samuel Wilberforce (1805-73) who owed his early success to just such royal favour

***rarae aves*:** (*Latin*) rare birds

Dr Whately: Richard Whately (1782-1863), a liberal Anglican who became Archbishop of Dublin in 1831. He supported religious toleration and political reform

Dr Hampden: Renn Dickson Hampden (1793-1868), Regius Professor of Divinity in the University of Oxford; Bishop of Hereford, 1847. He was a controversial figure whose views were opposed by traditionalists, and whose appointments were vigorously objected to

papists . . . dissenters: Roman Catholic and Protestants outside the Church of England had been penalised for their religion since the seventeenth century

high church principles: allegiance to the political and religious beliefs which distinguished the Church of England from other Protestant churches. They emphasised the authority of bishops and the necessity of the sacrament. Politically, they implied strong support for the Crown

Socinianism: a Christian heresy of the sixteenth century which denied the divinity of Christ

the Presbyterian Synods of Scotland and Ulster: an assembly of the clergymen of the Presbyterian Church which believed in government by clergymen and laymen rather than by the rule of bishops

regium donum: (*Latin*) royal gift – a grant to nonconformist clergymen in financial need

Maynooth grant: a controversial grant given by the government in 1845 to Maynooth College (St Patrick's College) in Ireland which had been founded in 1795 to train students for the Roman Catholic priesthood

Lambeth: the palace of the Archbishop of Canterbury in London

Bishopsthorpe: the palace of the Archbishop of York in York (actually, Bishopthorpe)

Sabbatarian rule: a strict observance of Sunday as a day of worship. Sunday travelling, especially by railway, was a frequent target of sabbatarians

the eyes of Argus: in Greek mythology, a giant with a hundred eyes

Chapter 4: The Bishop's Chaplain

Mr Slope was a graduate of Cambridge who had begun his career as a teacher and had then been moved to a recently built church in London where he had become a close friend of Mrs Proudie. He had fallen in love with one of the bishop's daughters but had allowed his affection to cool on learning that the bishop was not wealthy enough to provide her with a dowry. He hoped to wield considerable power in Barchester, although he knew Mrs Proudie meant to do so too. He was prepared to support the bishop, if necessary, to reduce her influence.

Mr Slope was an able man who knew how to use humility as a means to power. He was an effective preacher, impressing on his hearers the sinful state in which they lived. He was not likely to be in harmony with the habits of Barchester. He wanted to know what his parishioners were doing, wanted them to obey his rules of conduct and intended to reprove them if they did not. Ladies found him hard to resist, but he was not likely to be popular with the gentlemen of Barchester.

NOTES AND GLOSSARY:

that eminent physician who assisted at the birth of Mr T. Shandy: a reference to Dr Slop, a character in *Tristam Shandy*, the comic novel by Lawrence Sterne (1713-68)

sizar: a student in the University of Cambridge who receives an allowance towards his college expenses. Formerly he had certain services to perform

Wesleyan-Methodists: the tradition of Methodism associated with John Wesley (1703-91) which had much in common with the Evangelical movement in the Church of England

Puseyites: see Part 1 of these Notes, p. 11.

high-pitched roof . . . a full-breasted black . . . waistcoat . . . a book of prayer printed with red letters: associated with the revival of interest in the stricter interpretation of the doctrines of the Church of England was a movement to restore the beauty of its churches and a greater uniformity in the conduct of its services and the dress of its ministers. The 'red letters' referred to were the rubrics, or instruction for the conduct of services which were printed in red in the Prayer Book

that sermon which fell from divine lips: the Sermon on the Mount, see Matthew 5-7

Barchester Close: the houses round the Cathedral where the Cathedral clergy lived

prebendaries: clergymen in a cathedral who held a prebend, or stipend derived from the revenues of the Cathedral

minor canons: clergymen who assist in the cathedral services but are not members of the chapter

the Queen's supremacy in things spiritual: by the Act of Supremacy of 1534 the King and his successors were acknowledged as the spiritual head of the Church of England

Ernulfus: Bishop of Rochester (1040-1124). He is the author of a curse pronounced by Dr Slop in Sterne's *Tristram Shandy*

low church: the branch of the Church of England most affected by Evangelical enthusiasm

Chapter 5: A Morning Visit

Mr Harding, the former warden of Hiram's Hospital, expected to be reappointed to the post. He hoped his daughter, Eleanor, would go with him, though she wanted a home of her own where she could bring up her son. On the day after the bishop's arrival, Mr Harding went with his son-in-law, Archdeacon Grantly, to pay him a visit, only to find Mr Slope and Mrs Proudie sitting with the bishop in his room. Dr Grantly was greeted with the ceremony appropriate to his station; Mr Harding was given less attention. It was soon clear that the new bishop and his entourage would attempt to restrict the influence the archdeacon had enjoyed. Mrs Proudie patronised him and Mr Slope asked what arrangements had been made for the establishment of Sunday Schools. He also complained about Sunday travelling in Barchester. The two clergymen took their leave as politely as they could; neither felt satisfied with his reception.

NOTES AND GLOSSARY:

the palace: the common name in England for the residence of a bishop of archbishop

Dr Proudie was playing Venus to his Juno: in Greek mythology, the shepherd Paris was asked to judge which of the goddesses, Juno, Minerva or Venus, was the most beautiful and most worthy of the golden apple. Paris chose Venus, thus making the other two jealous

the hebdomadal council: a body established in 1854 to widen the government of Oxford University, until that time governed by the heads of colleges, collectively called the Hebdomadal Board

University Improvement Committee: a reference to one of the Committees for the Reform of Oxford University set up after the 1854 Oxford University Reform Act

Manufacturing Towns Morning and Evening Sunday School Society: another typical committee of the time set up to deal with the problem of providing religious instruction for the increased population of the new manufacturing towns

'Bradshaw': *Bradshaw's Railway Guide*, the standard Victorian railway timetable

'Neither thou, nor thy son, nor thy daughter, nor thy manservant, nor thy maidservant': the Fourth Commandment (Exodus 20: 10) is the basis for the strict observance of the Sabbath day, which Mrs Proudie is urging on Mr Harding

had I the pen of a mighty poet: the poet referred to is the Greek poet Homer whose *Iliad* opens with a reference to the wrath of Achilles

Chapter 6: War

Dr Grantly and Mr Harding agreed that they disliked Mr Slope and Mrs Proudie. It was clear to them that the bishop was merely a puppet in their hands. Dr Grantly believed he must oppose Mr Slope's influence: whatever Mr Slope disapproved of, Dr Grantly would support. Formal courtesies would have to be exchanged between Mrs Grantly and Mrs Proudie, but no further cordiality could be allowed to develop. Mr Slope began by thinking that he might win Dr Grantly to his side, but now he saw there could be no friendship between them. Given the opportunity of preaching in the Cathedral, on the day when the bishop was installed, Mr Slope lost no time in telling the clergy of the diocese how they should behave. The service had been very beautiful, the singing in particular having been well managed by Mr Harding. But Mr Slope had a low opinion of the beauty of church services. In his eyes what mattered was not the form of the service but the feelings and beliefs of the congregation. Believers should understand, rather than simply enjoy, the faith they professed to hold.

Mr Slope conveyed the impression that his views were shared by the bishop, though the bishop was terrified by his chaplain's outspokenness.

NOTES AND GLOSSARY:

Puseyite practices: the movement to reform the services of the Church of England took account of how clergymen should dress. White surplices, worn by the reformers, were resented by some congregations as a sign of Rome.

the science of intoning: the method of reciting the services in a singing voice

the real presence: the actual presence of Christ's body and blood in the sacrament of the Eucharist

brougham: a one-horse closed carriage, named after Lord Brougham (1778-1868)

***carte du pays*:** (*French*) the map of the country, the 'lie of the land'

the Hon. and Rev.: the prefix 'honourable' is given to the sons of peers below the rank of marquess. Charles, 3rd Earl of Stanhope (1753-1816) was an inventor and an open carriage called a 'Stanhope' was named after the historical Hon. and Rev. Fitzroy Stanhope (1787-1864)

Te Deum: an ancient Latin hymn of praise sung (in an English translation) at morning prayers in the Church of England

litany: the form of public prayer, set out in the Book of Common Prayer, in which the clergy lead and the people respond

the precepts addressed by St Paul to Timothy: see II Timothy 2: 15

high and dry church: see Part 1 of these Notes, p. 11

***parvenu*:** 'a person of obscure origin who has attained wealth or position beyond that of his class' (*Oxford English Dictionary*)

the old man whom we Sindbads cannot shake off: Sinbad (in *The Arabian Nights*) was forced to carry a monster, called the Old Man of the Sea, on his back

Hades: Hell

Chapter 7: The Dean and Chapter Take Counsel

Mr Slope's sermon caused great offence, though some people, who were pleased by novelty, thought there might be something in what he said. Even some of the clergy, who were aware of the benefits the bishop had it in his power to confer, were willing to be friends with his chaplain. The leading clergymen, however, were agreed that Mr Slope must not be allowed to preach in the cathedral again. Before long everybody in the town knew the chapter's opinion of Mr Slope's sermon. Bishop and Mrs Proudie thought it best to withdraw to London until the fuss was over. Mr Slope was left behind in Barchester to carry on his work. All Barchester was in a tumult.

NOTES AND GLOSSARY:

Gamaliel: the teacher of St Paul

Wilkes: John Wilkes (1725-97), English agitator and reformer who, despite his ugliness, was attractive to women

the loaves and fishes of the diocese of Barchester: the biblical parable of the loaves and fishes which fed five thousand (Mark 6: 37-44). Mr Slope is seen as one of the vessels in which the benefits miraculously provided for the clergy of Barchester are stored

the chancellor: one of the chief dignitaries of the Cathedral Chapter

some new Sion or Bethesda: names for Nonconformist chapels

Chapter 8: The Ex-Warden Rejoices in his Probable Return to the Hospital

---

Eleanor Bold and Mary Bold, her sister-in-law, had not been among the ladies of Barchester who had welcomed Mr Slope, but even they were more favourably disposed towards him after he had paid a visit to them one day. He warmly praised Mr Harding's musical ability and said things to the ladies which pleased them. Mr Harding was surprised that Mr Slope had managed to ingratiate himself with his daughter; he felt sure he had some special motive for doing so. Mr Harding was looking forward to returning to his old post in the Hospital, even although his salary would be reduced. He neither expected nor intended to be under an obligation to the new bishop for the position he had voluntarily resigned. Still less did he mean to be obliged to Mr Slope. Whatever Mr Slope had meant by his sermon, it was wrong of him to speak disrespectfully of the practices of his elders: no religious conviction obliged a man to be discourteous.

NOTES AND GLOSSARY:

want: distinguish want=need from want=lack. Thus 'as regards income I shall have plenty for all I want' but 'at my time of life there is a want of'

Chapter 9: The Stanhope Family

Among Bishop Proudie's reforms was the recall of clergymen who lived outside the diocese and left their duties to others. Dr Vesey Stanhope, for example, had lived in Italy for two years, giving poor health as an excuse. He returned to Barchester with his wife, son and two daughters. Dr Stanhope was not deeply devoted to the church; he was mainly interested in food and wine. His wife, who had been a beauty, was mainly concerned with her clothes. Their house was looked after by their elder daughter, Charlotte, who was a good manager, clever, but indifferent to religious matters. Her sister, Madeline, had been rather wild in her youth; she had married a poor Italian called Neroni, by whom she had a daughter. After a mysterious accident, she had returned to her father's house and had taken permanently to a sofa on which she received visitors. If she went out, she was carried to and from her carriage. She wrote poetry, read novels and carried on a correspondence with a large circle of friends. Their brother Ethelbert had found that neither the church nor the law interested him as a profession; he had decided to earn his living as an artist. Although he had talent, he did not apply himself. He dabbled in fashionable religious enthusiasms; he got into debt, and had to be rescued by his father. He worked as a sculptor in Italy but decided to return to England with the rest of the family. He was agreeable, unconventional and very ready to flirt, but had very little feeling for others or sense of principle. Despite his family's unconventionality, Dr Stanhope was well known in Barchester and of good standing. He had been a friend of Dr Grantly in their student days. All sides in the opposing church factions in Barchester looked to him as an ally.

NOTES AND GLOSSARY:

prebendal stall: the seat reserved for a canon of the cathedral
***bon vivant*:** (*French*) someone who likes living well
far niente (*Italian*) idleness
***trousseau*:** a bride's outfit of clothes
Grecian *bandeaux*: (*French*) narrow bands used by women to bind their hair in classical style
Lucifer: Satan, the leader of the angels who rebelled against God
basilisk: a monster in mythology whose look could kill
the worst of the Caesars: Nero (AD37-60), a notoriously depraved Roman Emperor
Judea: the southern part of Palestine, occupied by the Jewish community in post-exilic days under Persian, Greek and Roman overlordship

Moses: the great Jewish law-giver, prophet and leader

Messiah: the Hebrew title applied in the prophetic writings to a promised deliverer of the Jewish nation and applied to Jesus of Nazareth by his followers. Bertie Stanhope clearly considers that the 'true Messiah' has yet to appear

Sidonia: a Jewish financier who is a character in *Coningsby* (1844) by Benjamin Disraeli (1804-81)

Carrara: a town in Northern Italy famous for its marble

***mauvaise honte*:** (*French*) shyness

lords of whiggish tendency: at this time the terms Whig and Liberal, Tory and Conservative were used interchangeably

Chapter 10: Mrs Proudie's Reception – Commenced

After two months in London the Proudies returned to Barchester and held an evening party to which everybody of any social consequence in the neighbourhood was invited. Even Dr and Mrs Grantly, Mr Harding and Eleanor and Mary Bold decided to go. Dr Stanhope feared that the behaviour of his daughter, Signora Neroni, would be likely to shock the sober people of Barchester, but she, too, was determined to go. Mr Slope had made the arrangements for the evening. He had persuaded Mrs Proudie, rather against her will, to provide supper for her guests. The party was held in the upstairs rooms of the bishop's palace which had been converted for the purpose of entertaining. The signora's party was the last to arrive and her entrance caused a considerable stir. She was carried in by her brother and three servants, her sister following, and placed on a sofa. She was strikingly and magnificently dressed and drew every eye to her. It was not clear from his dress whether the Italian man-servant was a servant or a friend of the family. Having made the mistake of treating the servant as a guest, Dr Proudie made things worse by attempting to treat Bertie Stanhope as a servant. But Bertie soon corrected him.

Chapter 11: Mrs Proudie's Reception – Concluded

Bertie Stanhope quickly shook hands with Dr Proudie and began to ask him many personal questions about his promotion to the bishopric. Embarrassed by the questioning Dr Proudie made his way between the head of the signora's sofa and a large clergyman who had been blocking his path. Bertie asked the clergyman to help him to move the sofa and the sofa was propelled into the middle of the floor, where it tore away a considerable part of the train of Mrs Proudie's dress. Rushing to her side, Bertie knelt in an attempt to free the dress. He looked as if he was pleading for mercy and the scene was lucidrous enough to make the signora laugh. Thoroughly offended, Mrs Proudie left the room. Dr Proudie was outraged to discover at last that the signora and the impudent young man were the children of one of his subordinate clergy. But he had to admit the lady was an agreeable woman. Bertie continued to talk tactlessly, criticising the system of education at the University of Oxford. His bad manners broke up the conversation and the bishop pursued Mr Harding to ask if he was prepared to return to Hiram's Hospital. Pleased at the idea of his return, Mr Harding felt annoyed when the bishop asked him to discuss the matter with Mr Slope. Mr Slope, meanwhile, was sitting with the signora, much to Mrs Proudie's indignation. She was outraged at the attention he was paying the signora. The younger Stanhopes were the last to leave the party. Mrs Proudie was determined that the signora should never be asked again.

NOTES AND GLOSSARY:

Translations: the removal of a bishop from one see to another

They've cut them down: the stipends of bishops had been equalised by the Established Church Act of 1836

'I like the Church of Rome best': a tactless remark. Since 1845, a disquieting number of Church of England clergymen had left to become Roman Catholics

Gathers . . . stitches . . . plaits . . . flounces . . . breadths: all the intricate work that has gone into the creation of the dress is ruined, leaving only the plain material behind

embrasures . . . parapets . . . casemated stories: not for the first time the elaborate lady's dress of the period is compared to a fortress. Notice the mock-heroic language Trollope uses here in his imitation of an epic simile. Perhaps he is echoing *The Rape of the Lock* by Alexander Pope (1688-1744)

preferment: promotion

Tiberius: Emperor of Rome in AD14-37

the last of the Visigoths: the subject of *Roderick: the Last of the Goths* (1814) by Robert Southey (1774-1843)

the last of the Mohicans: the title of a novel by J. Fenimore Cooper (1789-1851)

***fortiter in re . . . suaviter in modo*:** (*Latin*) resolute in action, gentle in method

***omnium gatherum*:** a miscellaneous assemblage (a mock Latin phrase)

we have not been so hard upon you at Oxford: a reference to Bishop Proudie's membership of the University

Improvement Committee and its reform of the government of the University of Oxford (see note on Chapter 5, p. 21)

hebdomadal board: the unreformed Council of the Heads of Oxford Colleges which met weekly

German professors: English university education in the early years of the nineteenth century was often compared unfavourably to that in Germany

***ci-devant*:** (*French*) former

Chapter 12: Slope versus Harding

Two or three days later Mr Harding received from Mr Slope an ingratiating note asking him to call at the palace to discuss the question of the Hospital. As he waited for Mr Slope Mr Harding thought mournfully of all the pleasures of his life at Barchester which now seemed so out of tune with the new order of things. In these days he needed his religion more than ever. Mr Slope kept him waiting for some time, then spoke to him in a condescending way about the Hospital, his salary and his duties. Hitherto the hospital had been a sinecure, now it was to have a Sunday School for the benefit of the children of the poor; church services for the inmates of the hospital would be increased. It was not clear to Mr Harding whether the offer of the post was conditional upon his accepting these new duties. He told Mr Slope to tell the bishop he could not accept the post with new conditions. Mr Slope told the bishop that Mr Harding had refused it. Mrs Proudie suggested Mr Quiverful should be given the post. Mr Slope proposed that he would visit Mr Quiverful.

NOTES AND GLOSSARY:

sizarship: see note on Chapter 4, p. 19

Quiverful: for the significance of this clergyman's name, see the Bible, Psalm 127: 4-5

Chapter 13: The Rubbish Cart

Mr Harding did not feel that he had been well treated by Mr Slope. He could endure the loss of his position at the Hospital and the benefits which went with it, but he was not pleased to learn that he was no longer suited to the times. Was his life now to be regarded as worthless? If so, had he the strength of character to repent his shortcomings and seek a better life? He decided to consult his son-in-law, Dr Grantly, but he went first to tell his daughter, Eleanor, what had happened. Mr Slope had visited her the previous day to suggest that she might help with the Sunday School which was to be attached to the new Hospital. She did not like Mr Slope personally but she thought he was an active clergyman who might be useful in Barchester. When she saw her father, Eleanor knew that all was not well. He told her it was likely that he would decline the Hospital, and went off to visit Dr Grantly. He was sorry his daughter appeared not to disapprove sufficiently of Mr Slope. Dr and Mrs Grantly had no such liking for the chaplain: Mrs Grantly even expressed the fear that Mr Slope might intend to marry Eleanor. Eleanor had no such intention, though she did not feel as hostile to Mr Slope as the Grantlys did. For his part Mr Slope for the moment had no other motive than to make himself as popular as he could among the ladies of Barchester.

NOTES AND GLOSSARY:

cacoethes: an 'itch' to do something, especially, to write

St Bartholomew: one of the twelve apostles

St Sebastian: a third-century (?) Roman martyr, supposed to be an officer of the Emperor's guard. When it was discovered that he was a Christian, he was executed by archers. His martyrdom was a favourite subject for later religious paintings

St Lorenzo: a Roman deacon and martyr (*d.*258). According to legend, he was roasted on a gridiron

a fly: a light carriage for hire

Chapter 14: The New Champion

That evening Archdeacon Grantly was able to tell his wife that Mr Arabin had agreed to become vicar of St Ewold's, a parish which lay just outside Barchester. Mr Arabin was a fellow of an Oxford College, a scholar and a gentleman; he was about forty years of age and unmarried. Dr Grantly, whose responsibility it was to fill the post, had decided that Mr Arabin was a suitable candidate because he had been active in defending the doctrines of the Church of England, and had engaged in public debate with Mr Slope on a disputed point of faith. Dr Grantly was delighted that he had been persuaded to accept the position and looked forward to having him as an ally against Slope. He was less pleased to hear from Mr Harding about the new conditions which appeared to have been attached to the wardenship of the hospital. While his own inclination was to challenge the bishop's power to alter the duties, Mr Harding's was to decline the post. Dr Grantly's view of the matter prevailed, and he went to bed in high good humour. It was then that his wife told him of her fear that Eleanor might consider marrying Mr Slope.

NOTES AND GLOSSARY:

fellow of Lazarus: a fellow is one of a group of scholars who, together with their head, constitute a college and are paid from its revenues

at all points: in every particular

the cesspool of Rome: this language is typical of the horror felt at the time for those who chose to leave the Church of England for the Church of Rome

temporalities: the property and revenues of the Church

spiritualities: the religious and spiritual values of the Church

apostolic succession: the question of the validity of the title of Anglican clergymen which was traced back to the apostles and held to derive from them by uninterrupted descent through successive bishops

the fellow of a college is never married: because Oxford Colleges had originally been monastic foundations, fellows were at this time still expected to resign from their fellowships if they married

The frogs and the mice . . . the angers of Agamemnon: reference to ecclesiastical disputes. The second dispute referred to is the subject of Homer's *Iliad*, the first is to a parody of Greek epic, formerly attributed to Homer, called *A Battle between the Frogs and the Mice*. The debate between Mr Arabin and Mr Slope is placed somewhere between these two encounters

Chapter 15: The Widow's Suitors

When Mr Slope went to discuss Hiram's Hospital with Mr Quiverful, he learned for the first time that Mr Harding's widowed daughter was a rich woman. Mr Quiverful was a poor man with fourteen children, but he was very unwilling to consider the wardenship unless he was sure that Mr Harding had refused it; Mr Slope assured him that he had. But the news that Eleanor Bold was wealthy made Mr Slope hesitate. If Mrs Bold now seemed an attractive prospect as Mr Slope's wife, why should his prospective father-in-law not be provided for also? But Mr Slope's desire for Mrs Bold's money was tempered by his dislike for Dr Grantly and by his admiration for the beauty of Signora Neroni. Signora Neroni was a married woman: Mr Slope's admiration for her cost him some pangs of conscience. He wondered whether his duty might not lie in the pursuit of Mrs Bold's money. Meanwhile Charlotte Stanhope was suggesting to her brother that marriage with Mrs Bold could solve his financial problems.

NOTES AND GLOSSARY:

a young raven: see Psalm 147:9 and Luke 12:24

Sufficient for the day is the evil thereof: see Matthew 6:34

***Cela dépend*:** (*French*) that depends

'And that a very little one, as the maid-servant said': so an illegitimate baby was excused in *Mr Midshipman Easy* (1836) by Captain Marryat (1792-1848)

lots of tin: (*slang*) money

the sacrifice of a Hindu woman at the burning of her husband's body: a supposed example of wifely devotion, known as 'suttee', in which the living woman was burned to death at the funeral of her husband

those horrid she-helmets: the widow's cap had a long veil which was gradually shortened during the period of widowhood

the third volume: nineteenth-century novels were conventionally published in three volumes

Mrs Ratcliffe's solemn curtain: in *The Mysteries of Udolpho* (1794) by Mrs Ann Radcliffe (1764-1823) frequent reference is made to a mysterious black veil

let the spectator never mistake the Syracusan for the Ephesian: the two pairs of twin brothers in *The Comedy of Errors* by Shakespeare, on whose mistaken identity the plot turns

Chapter 16: Baby Worship

Though Eleanor Bold was not so striking in appearance as Signora Neroni, she was a beautiful woman. She was very fond of her baby, and it was while she was playing with him that Mr Slope made his next visit. He had decided to pursue his interest in Eleanor and he tried to persuade the bishop to reconsider Mr Harding's position. By this time, however, Mrs Proudie had told Mrs Quiverful that her husband was to have the post. The bishop was afraid of his wife's opposition, if he changed his mind, but Mr Slope wished to encourage him to assert his authority. Mr Slope tried to explain to Eleanor that her father had appeared to refuse the post because new conditions had been attached to it, and the offer had now been made to Mr Quiverful, but he promised he would do his best to further her father's interests. He spoke much of his wish to be friends with the people of Barchester and to gain their sympathy and love. Eleanor was unaware that his words were meant specially for her. She was not sure whether Mr Slope could be trusted. She feared her father had lost the chance of returning to the hospital.

NOTES AND GLOSSARY:

dawty: darling, pet

simmered: murmured in a subdued voice

Rubens: Sir Peter Paul Rubens (1577-1640), the Flemish painter famous for his robustly voluptuous nudes

asphodel: a flower that in classical writing was said to cover the fields in the Land of the Blest

great big rough romping school: an English public (that is, private) school for boys is meant here. They were well known at this time for the violence of their pupils and teachers

***de trop*:** (*French*) unwanted

Chapter 17: Who shall be Cock of the Walk?

The bishop of Barchester did not feel happy about the way his wife interfered in the affairs of the diocese. Hitherto she had been supported by Mr Slope; now in the matter of Mr Harding's appointment, he seemed likely to oppose her. Perhaps this would give the bishop an opportunity to recover his authority. He invited Archdeacon Grantly to discuss the matter with him. He tried to persuade Mrs Proudie that Mr Harding should have this old post back, pointing out that Mr Slope now agreed with him. She said that the Quiverfuls expected to have it, since Mr Harding had refused it. The bishop retreated, but Mrs Proudie was indignant at Mr Slope's presumption. That evening she visited the chaplain in his room. She had not been pleased with his unduly attentive behaviour to Signora Neroni, and she told him so. She also told him that he was too inclined to give advice to the bishop. She left Mr Slope in no doubt about where such advice might best come from. It was clear to him that in the contest for influence over the bishop, either he or she must prevail.

NOTES AND GLOSSARY:

***Cock of the Walk*:** the dominant bully or master spirit

crossing a note: letters were 'crossed' when part of a page, already filled with writing, was used again transversely for further writing

Bob Acres: in *The Rivals* (1775) by Richard Brinsley Sheridan (1751-1816), he is a character celebrated for his country manners, his outlandish oaths, and his cowardice

the apron: part of the official dress of the bishop

I'll Slope him: a menace of incalculable force. A proper name used in this way implies that all the defects of the

	named individual's character will be used as weapons against him
the prelatess:	an ironic name for the bishop's wife

Chapter 18: The Widow's Persecution

Next day the bishop pleaded illness and asked Mr Slope to tell Dr Grantly that the wardenship was to be given to Mr Quiverful. He implied that this was the last time he would allow himself to be overruled by his wife. The archdeacon refused to see Mr Slope. Eleanor annoyed the archdeacon by telling him she had spoken to Mr Slope the previous day. He left her in no doubt that he disapproved of her behaviour. He still suspected she might be fond of Mr Slope, though the thought had not entered her head. She was angry that an action she thought might have helped her father should be disapproved of. The anger between his daughter and his son-in-law distressed Mr Harding. If Eleanor intended to marry Mr Slope, he would have to put up with it, since he loved his daughter deeply. He could not believe that Mr Slope's attitude about the wardenship could have changed so soon. Dr Grantly was convinced that Mr Slope intended to marry Eleanor. Mr Harding believed he should abandon any idea of returning to the hospital, but Dr Grantly wrote a strong note to the bishop pressing his father-in-law's claim. He suggested that Mr Harding and Eleanor should come to stay for a time at Plumstead, so that she could be out of Mr Slope's way. Mr Arabin, who was to be at Plumstead, might be able to advise them. Eleanor had been invited to visit the Stanhopes the following day, but she said she would be delighted to go to Plumstead the day after.

NOTES AND GLOSSARY:

***sotto voce*:**	(*Italian*) in an undertone
***tartuffe*:**	a religious hypocrite, after the character in the comedy of that name by the French dramatist Molière (1622-73)
***beaux yeux*:**	(*French*) beautiful eyes

Chapter 19: Barchester by Moonlight

The Stanhope family were not the most fortunate in the world: Dr Stanhope had never saved from his large income and his family were likely to be badly off when he died. His elder daughter was becoming an old maid; his younger daughter had been left a cripple; his son was a wastrel. His wife cared for little except clothes. Yet they did not complain about their fate. They were not sustained by any religious feeling; it was their lack of feeling which helped them endure their lot. On the day of Dr Grantly's visit to the bishop, Dr Stanhope was upset by some bills which had been incurred by the signora and by Bertie. Dr Stanhope made it plain to his son that he was angry, but Charlotte mollified him by holding out the prospect of a favourable marriage for Bertie. That evening Eleanor paid her promised visit. They made her welcome, but she was surprised to find that Mr Slope was expected too. He was not well pleased to find Eleanor and the signora together. The signora welcomed him in a confidential way which he found embarrassing, since he now believed he had shown to Eleanor that he cared for her. Eleanor was perfectly content to talk to Bertie Stanhope, who knew how to make himself agreeable. Later, Charlotte suggested that Eleanor, Bertie, Mr Slope and herself should stroll round the cathedral in the moonlight. Bertie escorted Eleanor; Charlotte went with Mr Slope. As they paused to admire the buildings of the Hospital, Eleanor was embarrassed by Bertie's asking when her father was to return to it. Later, she told him privately how matters stood. When they returned, Mr Slope was soon engrossed in confidential chat with the signora. Eleanor was left alone with Bertie who was agreeable and amusing. When Eleanor went home she felt the Stanhopes were the most agreeable family she had ever met.

NOTES AND GLOSSARY:

the Stoics: followers of the Greek philosopher Zeno (335-263BC) who believed in the repression of emotion, indifference to pleasure and pain and in the virtue of patient endurance

Dr Stanhope spoke of the custom of his youth: until 1838 it had been possible for debtors to be arrested for debt before the fact of their debt had been established in court. Compare, for example, the experience of Rawdon Crawley in *Vanity Fair* (1848) by W.M. Thackeray

wine-warrants: 'a warrant authorizing the delivery of wine from bond' (*Oxford English Dictionary*)

the chaste goddess: Diana, Roman goddess of the moon, was a virgin

Whewellite, Brewsterite, or t'othermanite: a reference to a contemporary debate between William Whewell (1794-1866) and David Brewster (1781-1868) about the possibility of life elsewhere in the universe. In *The Plurality of Worlds* (1853) Whewell argued that our world is 'the only one inhabited by sentient beings; in *More Worlds than One* (1854) Brewster took the other view

sidereal: concerning the stars

Chapter 20: Mr Arabin

It has already been mentioned that Mr Arabin was forty and unmarried. He was the younger son of a country gentleman, and had been educated at Winchester and at Balliol College, Oxford, where he had excelled in debate. He was deeply influenced by the Oxford Movement and by John Henry Newman. He graduated without special distinction because he had given too much of his energy to the service of his religious beliefs. But his qualities of mind outshone those of men with more impressive degrees. He gained a Fellowship at Lazarus College which was glad to welcome this defender of the Church. For a time he seemed in danger of following Newman into Roman Catholicism, the rigorous demands of which he found attractive. It was fortunate for his career that a humble clergyman of the Church of England taught him that the light of his own conscience was the surest guide for a Christian priest. Mr Arabin returned to his Fellowship at Oxford, recovered his self-confidence and became well-known as a preacher and controversialist, though his time of trial had given him a new humility of spirit. He was still pleasant-looking, witty but not ill-natured. He had not hitherto considered marriage, though he was popular with women. He did not at first impress Mrs Grantly or her daughters: on first acquaintance he often seemed shy. Mr Arabin had begun to regret his single-minded pursuit of an academic and clerical career. He had failed to form any permanent bonds and had despised the good things of life. Now he was poor and lonely.

NOTES AND GLOSSARY:

daguerrotype: an early form of photography invented by Louis Daguerre (1789-1851)

***labor omnia vincit improbus*:** (*Latin*) persistent labour overcomes all things. From the *Georgics*, 1, 145 by the Roman poet Virgil (70-19BC)

Winchester: one of the greatest of English public schools founded in 1387 by William of Wykeham. Trollope attended the school for a time as a boy

New College: Oxford college which was also founded by William of Wykeham. Trollope's father hoped one of his sons would win a scholarship to it, as he had done himself

commoner: an Oxford undergraduate who has gained entrance to the University without winning a scholarship to it

Balliol: an Oxford college founded by Sir John de Baliol in 1263

little go: the popular name for the first examination for the degree of BA
schism: a breach in the unity of the church
Froude's *Remains*: the *Remains*, or posthumous papers, of Hurrell Froude (1803-36) was a key document in the history of the Oxford Movement. It revealed the often rather hysterical attitudes of one of Newman's friends to the Church of England, the Reformation and Roman Catholicism
***éclat*:** (*French*) brilliant success
Tractarians: see Part 1, page 11
Newman: John Henry Newman, the leader of the Oxford Movement, was received into the Roman Catholic Church in 1845. He was a famous preacher in the University Church of St Mary the Virgin
double first: a place in the first class in each of the two final examinations at a University in two subjects
the waters of Jordan: in II Kings 5 the prophet Elisha commanded Naaman to bathe in the waters of Jordan so that his leprosy might be cured. Naaman thought the command was too simple
apostasy: the abandonment of one's religious or moral faith
Thirty-nine Articles: the thirty-nine statements of belief to which Church of England clergymen were required to subscribe
enthusiasm: often used to mean (especially in the eighteenth century) 'ill-regulated or misdirected religious emotion'
***façon de parler*:** (*French*) a manner of speaking
Exeter Hall: a public hall in London very often used by Evangelicals for their meetings

Chapter 21: St Ewold's Parsonage

Although Mrs Grantly and Eleanor Bold were sisters, they were too far apart in age to be close to one another. Mrs Grantly did not feel she could ask Eleanor directly if she liked Mr Slope. She was surprised to find that he had been at the Stanhopes' when Eleanor was there. She began to be convinced that the relationship between Eleanor and Mr Slope should be taken seriously. The archdeacon was even inclined to believe that Eleanor was being deceitful about her feelings for him. Eleanor could not help feeling that the Grantlys were less lively than the Stanhopes. Next day the whole party went off to visit the parsonage at St Ewold's. Eleanor found Mr Arabin more relaxed and humorous than she had expected: he found her more intelligent. The Grantlys were concerned about the physical state of the vicarage. Mr Arabin felt he was too poor to improve the place. Mrs Grantly believed alterations were best left to a woman. Someday Mr Arabin might have a wife with views on the subject – and she might have money to put them into effect.

NOTES AND GLOSSARY:

***savoir vivre*:** (*French*) knowledge of the world

dilapidations: the sums of money charged against a clergyman to make good damage done during the time he has occupied his church or vicarage

bradawl: a small boring-tool

'Let dogs delight to bark and bite': from *Divine Songs for Children* by Isaac Watts (1674-1748)

leaving a cloth on the table: traditionally, the cloth was *removed* from the table as a signal for the ladies to leave the gentlemen to their wine after dinner

***parvenu*:** (used here as an adjective) vulgar, ostentatious

dissenters: people who dissociate themselves from the Established Church of England

Chapter 22: The Thornes of Ullathorne

Mr Arabin conducted his first service at St Ewold's the next Sunday; Dr Grantly assisted him and Eleanor accompanied them. They were to lunch with the local squire, Wilfred Thorne of Ullathorne, a bachelor of about fifty, who still took pride in his appearance. Mr Thorne was a cultivated and deeply conservative gentleman; he admired the literature of the previous two centuries and did not care for publications of his own time. He was deeply versed in the history of the principal families of the county, including his own, which he was able to trace back to before the Norman Conquest. He was willing to respect wealth and talent, but pedigree was the mark of the gentleman. He had been pleased to find that Mr Arabin was connected to an ancient family, even although it no longer possessed its lands. In politics, Mr Thorne was a Tory who believed that the party had betrayed its principles when it took up Free Trade. This sense of political betrayal had affected his social life: for a time he even gave up hunting. He lived at Ullathorne with his older sister whose attitudes were even more conservative. The Thornes' house had been built in Tudor times: if it lacked some modern comforts, it had grandeur. Though the fireplace in the great hall which served as a dining-room had been adapted to burn coal, Miss Thorne would have preferred to burn logs there. Miss Thorne's drawing-room and Mr Thorne's study were pleasant modern rooms: beyond lay a decorative, well-kept garden, which was one of the chief attractions of the house. Opposite the gates lay St Ewold's church.

NOTES AND GLOSSARY:

Squire Western: the jovial, fox-hunting, prejudiced and irascible country squire in *Tom Jones* (1749) by Henry Fielding (1707-54)

Montaigne and Burton: Michel de Montaigne (1533-92), the famous French essayist. Robert Burton (1577-1640), the author of *The Anatomy of Melancholy* (1621). Both writers were reflective lovers of curious learning

complete sets of . . . the *Rambler*: each of these names was the title of a periodical published in the eighteenth century. This type of publication, consisting largely of essays, began with the *Tatler* (1709-11) and the *Spectator* (1711-14) written by Joseph Addison (1672-1719) and Richard Steele (1672-1729). It was continued by the *Rambler* (1750-2) and the *Idler* (1761) written by Samuel Johnson (1709-84)

Edinburgh and Quarterlies: *The Edinburgh Review* (founded 1802) was a Whig periodical; *the Quarterly Review* (founded 1804) was Tory

Cedric the Saxon: the Saxon landowner in *Ivanhoe* (1820) by Sir Walter Scott (1771-1832)

Ealfried: this form of the name is Old English (Saxon)

Geoffrey de Burgh: this name is Norman-French

King John: (1167-1216). During his reign which began in 1199, Magna Carta, the great charter of English liberty, was extorted from the king by his barons in 1215

Sophocles: Greek dramatist (496-406BC)

James I: (1566-1625). Son of Mary Queen of Scots, James became King of Scotland in 1567 and King of England in 1603. He instituted the order of baronetcy, the lowest degree of hereditary honour in Britain, in 1611

Fitzgeralds and De Burghs: once more the names are French. Mr Thorne appears to regard himself as one of the characters in Scott's *Ivanhoe*, a native Saxon oppressed by the invading French

ichor: the ethereal fluid supposed to flow like blood in the veins of the gods

fifty-three Trojans: fifty-three diehard Tories still voted against Free Trade as late as 1852

Mr Dod: C.P.R. Dod (1793-1855), editor of *The Parliamentary Companion*

the repeal of the corn laws: until the middle of the nineteenth century a set of laws forbade the importation of foreign grain except under conditions which were carefully regulated to protect the revenues of British farmers. The laws were repealed in 1846 after much public agitation

Sir Robert Peel: the English Tory Prime Minister (1788-1850) whose conversion to Free Trade led to the repeal of the Corn Laws and the disarray of the Tory Party of the day

Eleusinian mysteries: religious rites in honour of Greek corn goddesses

palladium: originally, the wooden statue of Pallas in the citadel of Troy, on the preservation of which the city depended. Now, anything on which the safety of a people is supposed to depend

Cato: Marcius Porcius Cato (95-46BC) a Roman statesman whose name was associated with a devotion to liberty and the right

hope of a garter: the Most Noble Order of the Garter is the highest order of knighthood in Great Britain

Addison . . . Fielding: Joseph Addison, Jonathan Swift (1667-1745), Richard Steele: famous writers for the periodicals of the eighteenth century; Daniel Defoe (1660-1731), Henry Fielding: eighteenth-century novelists

Dryden: John Dryden (1631-1700), poet, essayist and playwright

***The Rape of the Lock*:** famous mock-heroic poem (1714) by Dryden's successor, Alexander Pope

Spenser: Edmund Spenser (1552-99) was the author of *The Faerie Queene* (1590-6), an allegorical romance dedicated to Queen Elizabeth

Hengist, Horsa: leaders of the first settlement by the Jutes in Britain in the fifth century AD

Scott's Ulrica: a prophetess in the novel *Ivanhoe* by Sir Walter Scott

Mista, Skogula . . . Zernebock: Saxon gods invoked by her against the Norman noblemen

Reform Bill: in 1832 a major reform of the system of parliamentary representation was carried through against much opposition

Catholic Emancipation: in 1829 the Duke of Wellington (1769-1852) removed the civil disabilities from which Roman Catholics still suffered
Lord Eldon: John Scott, Earl of Eldon (1731-1838), a deeply conservative Lord Chancellor (1801-27)
Druidess: the Druids were a pre-Christian order of priests in Celtic Britain
St Augustine: the founder of the Christian Church in Southern England, and first Archbishop of Canterbury (*d.*604)
Cranmer: Thomas Cranmer (1489-1556), Archbishop of Canterbury (1533). Executed in 1556, he was regarded as a Protestant martyr
Stuart: the royal house of Stuart which lost the throne after the exile of James II in 1688 and failed to regain it in the rebellions of 1715 and 1745
the lady of Branksome: in *The Lay of the Last Minstrel* (1805) by Sir Walter Scott
mullions: vertical stone bars in windows
oriel: a recess with a window projecting from a wall
Lely . . . Kneller: Sir Peter Lely (1618-80), Sir Godfrey Kneller (1646?-1723): fashionable portrait painters
Pan: the Greek god of flocks and shepherds

Chapter 23: Mr Arabin Reads Himself in at St Ewold's

Mr Arabin was rather shy among his new parishioners. He and his friends arrived first at Ullathorne Court and were welcomed by the Thornes. Then they walked to the church, where Mr Arabin was introduced to some of his principal parishioners. He read the lessons and preached a sermon on the combined Christian doctrines of faith and good works. Afterwards the party lunched at Ullathorne Court, where Miss Thorne was especially attentive to Eleanor, enquiring about the childish ailments of her little boy and offering strong views about the doctors of Barchester, while the archdeacon talked about farming matters to the squire. In the afternoon Mr Arabin read the lessons and the archdeacon preached a sermon welcoming Mr Arabin to his new charge.

NOTES AND GLOSSARY:
***mauvaise honte*:** see note on Chapter 9
churchwardens . . . severe: a reference to the churchwardens' traditional duty to report the clergyman to the bishop for any breach of church law

Dominie Sampson: in *Guy Mannering* (1815) by Sir Walter Scott, a learned but unworldly man who failed to become a minister and remained a schoolmaster
absolution: the formula used in church for declaring that sins are forgiven
coshered up: pampered, treated with fondness
coral: a toy made of polished coral, given to infants to help them cut their teeth
Daffy's Elixir: a soothing syrup for children
succedaneum: a substitute
guano: a fertiliser made from the droppings of sea-birds on the coast of South America
naiad . . . dryad: water-nymph; wood-nymph

Chapter 24: Mr Slope Manages Matters Very Cleverly at Puddingdale

During the next two weeks the visitors to Plumstead had an enjoyable time. Dinner parties were given by the Grantlys for the Thornes and by the Thornes for the Grantlys. The Grantlys and their guests had also been invited to the Stanhopes: Mr Arabin had received the attention the signora gave to all men. Eleanor had not quite liked this, though she had been pleasantly entertained by Bertie Stanhope. She liked Mr Arabin, but felt he did not take her seriously enough. But life at Plumstead went on pleasantly until something happened to disturb the harmony. It came about as follows. Mr Slope had now decided that his interests would best be served by an attempt to persuade Mr Quiverful to give up the wardenship in favour of Mr Harding. He went to Puddingdale to attempt to persuade Mr Quiverful that a mistake had been made. The prospect of the appointment meant much to Mr Quiverful and his family; he was too poor to think it dishonourable to seek Mr Slope's favour. Despite his disappointment he soon came to terms with Mr Slope's change of mind. He gave Mr Slope an assurance that he resigned any claim he might have to the wardenship.

NOTES AND GLOSSARY:

'How beautiful upon the mountains are the feet of him that bringeth good tidings': Isaiah 52:7

Chapter 25: Fourteen Arguments in Favour of Mr Quiverful's Claims

Mrs Quiverful was not so easily put off. She felt her husband had been too soft. Her family's debts could not wait until the bishop had something else to offer. She was at first inclined to believe that Mrs Proudie had betrayed her. Her husband's report of what Mr Slope had said then suggested to her that Mrs Proudie might not know what had happened, and therefore she sought an interview with the bishop's wife. It was soon evident that Mrs Proudie did not know about Mr Slope's visit to Puddingdale and that she and Mr Slope were no longer allies. When she heard what Mrs Quiverful had to say, Mrs Proudie marched off to see the bishop.

NOTES AND GLOSSARY:

Medea: in Greek legend Medea is better known for murdering her two children by Jason the leader of the Argonauts

Constance: the mother of young Arthur in *King John* by Shakespeare

Theseus . . . Amazon: Theseus was a legendary king of Athens who defeated the Amazons, a tribe of female warriors. He married their queen, Hippolyta

'an excellent thing in woman': this is how Lear describes his daughter's voice in Shakespeare's *King Lear*, V. 3. 273

scream out trumpet-tongued to the ears of men: see Shakespeare, *Macbeth*, I. 7. 19-20

E'en such a man, so faint, so spiritless . . . : Shakespeare, *Henry IV, Part Two*, I. 1. 70-72

under the rose: secretly (Latin, *sub rosa*)

tax-cart: a two-wheeled open cart, taxed at a reduced rate

sesquipedalian: lengthy

James Fitzplush: name for a footman, derived from Thackeray's character (see note on Chapter 1)

Chapter 26: Mrs Proudie Wrestles and Gets a Fall

When Mrs Proudie – without knocking – made her way into her husband's room, she found him with Mr Slope. Mr Slope explained that Mr Quiverful had now abandoned his claim to the hospital. Mrs Proudie told Mr Slope he should not interfere. Mr Slope said there would be much ill-feeling in Barchester, if Mr Harding's claims were ignored. Mrs Proudie said Mr Slope had misunderstood Mr Quiverful and she asked who had sent him to Puddingdale. Mr Slope said he owed a duty only to the bishop. Mrs Proudie invited him to leave the room. In the pause that followed, Mrs Proudie asked the bishop which of them was to go. The bishop said he and Mr Slope were busy. Mr Slope could not help looking triumphant as Mrs Proudie left. Mrs Proudie returned to tell Mrs Quiverful that, since her husband had relinquished the hospital, there was nothing more to be done. Thinking of her children, Mrs Quiverful wept, and Mrs Proudie assured her that she would do all in her power to see that Mr Quiverful got his promised promotion.

NOTES AND GLOSSARY:

tête-à-tête: (*French*) private talk

flesh of her flesh and bone of her bone: a corruption of the way Eve was described by Adam (Genesis 2: 23)

Achilles: Greek hero of the Trojan war

Don Quixote: hero of the romance of the same name by Miguel de Cervantes (1547-1616). He believed he had been called to put right the wrongs of the world

Chapter 27: A Love Scene

Mr Slope wrote a letter to Mrs Bold, telling her that Mr Quiverful had given up his claim to the wardenship and suggesting that Mr Harding should go to the bishop. The letter had some phrases which suggested a greater intimacy with Eleanor than was the case. Having delivered it to Eleanor's house, where he was told it would be delivered to Plumstead, Mr Slope paid a call on the signora, although he knew the many reasons why he should keep away from her. The signora had no feeling for Mr Slope but enjoyed the sense of power his admiration gave her. She was well aware that Mr Slope's real interests lay in marrying Eleanor, and advised him not to mix love with business. Love in the signora's opinion was an idle dream. She made light of Mr Slope's professed indifference to wealth. She challenged him to tell her he loved her and when he did so, she asked him when he intended to marry Eleanor Bold. When he denied any such intention, the signora asked him how he would feel if she, a hopeless cripple, were to return his love. So far as he was concerned, she considered her self free to marry – she had divorced Signor Neroni in her heart. Surely Mr Slope would not sacrifice all hope of wordly advancement for her? Their conversation was interrupted by the arrival of Mrs Stanhope and Mr Slope went home with a troubled conscience.

NOTES AND GLOSSARY:

It's gude to be off with the auld luve: old Scots song quoted in full in Chapter 46

two strings to Cupid's bow: being in love with two people at the same time

Convocation: an historical assembly of the Church of England which had formerly attempted to assert an exclusive right to consider church affairs under the direction of the Crown. This right had been disputed by Parliament and no meeting of

Convocation had been held since 1717. Attempts were made to revive these assemblies in the nineteenth century

Euclid: a mathematician of Alexandria, who flourished *c.*300BC. His works were still used as textbooks in nineteenth-century schools

Dido: in Virgil's (see note on chapter 20, p. 34) *Aeneid*, Dido, Queen of Carthage, is deserted by Aeneas

Cleopatra: in *Anthony and Cleopatra* (1600-7) by Shakespeare Cleopatra insisted on going with Antony to the sea-battle at Actium, but at the height of battle she deserted him

Nemesis: the personification of Justice in Greek mythology

Juliet: in *Romeo and Juliet* by Shakespeare

Haidee: in *Don Juan* (1819-24) by Lord Byron (1788-1824)

Troilus: the Trojan hero of *Troilus and Cressida* by Shakespeare; he was deserted by Cressida

Imogen . . . Desdemona . . . Ophelia: heroines respectively of Shakespeare's *Cymbeline* (1610), *Othello* (1604) and *Hamlet* (1603), who were badly treated by their lovers

the fruit of the Dead Sea: apples supposed to be beautiful outside, but full of ashes inside

Philidor: François Philidor (1726-95), a French composer and chess-player

première jeunesse: (*French*) first youth

boody: mope, be sullen

Chapter 28: Mrs Bold is Entertained by Dr and Mrs Grantly at Plumstead

That afternoon, when Dr Grantly and Mr Harding called at Eleanor's house to collect some parcels for her, they were given Mr Slope's letter. Dr Grantly recognised his handwriting and was disgusted to think that he was in correspondence with Eleanor. He was convinced it was a love-letter. When they reached Plumstead, Mr Harding gave Eleanor the note. She read it with pleasure for her father's sake, though she did not care for the references to herself. At dinner, there was a noticeable coolness, even from Mr Arabin, to whom Dr Grantly had confided what he believed were Eleanor's feelings for Mr Slope. Mrs Grantly tried to discuss the matter with Eleanor, who resented such an intrusion into her private affairs. She showed the letter to her father who was disgusted that Mr Slope had intervened in the matter. He did not wish to owe Mr Slope a favour. He assumed that the references to Eleanor meant that she had encouraged Slope. Had any discussion of her feelings taken place, Eleanor would have made it clear she did not like him. She did not suspect what the others thought; she was too sensitive to express her own distaste at Mr Slope's vulgarity. When her father left her, a message came from the archdeacon. He asked Eleanor to go to see him in his study.

NOTES AND GLOSSARY:

***billet-doux*:** (*French*) love letter
***particeps criminis*:** (*Latin*) accomplice
laches: culpable negligence (*Oxford English Dictionary*)
trepanned: ensnared, cheated
Lucretia . . . Tarquin: Sextus Tarquinius, the son of the last Roman king, is alleged to have raped his cousin Lucretia: the subject of a poem by Shakespeare
penetralia: (originally *Latin*) the innermost parts of a building (especially a sanctuary, a shrine)
freemasonry: a secret fraternity with its own ritual
go on all fours: to be on equal terms with
the cloth was drawn: a sign for the ladies to leave the men to their wine
the Cholera: serious outbreaks of cholera had taken place in 1831

Chapter 29: A Serious Interview

Against his wife's advice, Dr Grantly had decided it was his duty to tell Eleanor she had behaved improperly in receiving a letter from Mr Slope. Eleanor said the letter was about her father. She accused Dr Grantly of thinking the worst of Mr Slope. Dr Grantly warned her she was in danger of losing her friends, and that Mr Arabin agreed with the Grantlys that Eleanor could never come to Plumstead as Mr Slope's wife. Eleanor was outraged at Dr Grantly's impertinence. She thought Mr Arabin must have been responsible for the suggestion that she might marry Mr Slope. Dr Grantly complained to his wife that he thought Eleanor was proud of Mr Slope's affection for her. He did not see how he could continue to welcome her as a guest. Next day, after urging her father to go to see the bishop, Eleanor hurried back to Barchester.

NOTES AND GLOSSARY:

Mercury: in Roman mythology, the messenger of the gods.

Chapter 30: Another Love Scene

When Mr Arabin began to consider the possibility of Eleanor's being in love with Mr Slope, he found he regretted she was about to throw herself away on a man he despised. When he thought of her sweetness, her intelligence, her interest in the church and in himself, he could not believe she could marry Slope. He was too troubled in mind to do anything useful at St Ewold's. He went back to Plumstead to see her. She was sitting with her father in the drawing-room, but after some trite remarks, her father left them together. Eleanor accused him of lack of charity. He had spoken ill of her to Dr Grantly. Mr Arabin tried to repeat what he and Dr Grantly had talked about. Eleanor would not listen. She said she was accused of wanting to marry Mr Slope, because she had not treated him with the hostility expected of her. She left Mr Arabin to think about what she had said. He realised he loved her and, following her, found her still angry and reproachful. He could not openly declare his love for her, and she refused to help him to do so. He asked her if she intended to marry Mr Slope: she would not answer. She said he had no right to ask her. After lunch she left Plumstead without seeing him again.

NOTES AND GLOSSARY:

Van Artevelde: Hero of *Philip Van Artevelde* (1834), a play by Henry Taylor (1800-86); the lines that follow are a quotation from this play

Lord Tattenham Corner: a fictitious name derived from a point on the race-course at Epsom on which the Derby is run

Lothario: a seducer of women, from a tragedy called *The Fair Penitent* (1703) by Nicholas Rowe (1674-1718)

Chapter 31: The Bishop's Library

Within a few days of Eleanor's departure the party at Plumstead had broken up and Barchester had been agitated by the news of the illness of Dr Trefoil, the dean of Barchester, who had suffered a stroke. There was little hope of his recovery. The clergymen of Barchester gathered in the library to discuss the dean's health and the probable income of his successor. Was it possible that Mr Slope might become dean of Barchester? The dean rallied a little: for the next eight or ten days he remained semi-conscious.

Chapter 32: A New Candidate for Ecclesiastical Honours

Mr Slope and Mrs Proudie had not met since the day the bishop refused to ask Mr Slope to leave his study. For a time the bishop had enjoyed the pleasure of being master in his own house but Mrs Proudie reasserted her authority in private. The bishop was in a chastened frame of mind when Mr Slope came to announce the illness of the dean. That night Mr Slope began to think of his own chances of promotion. The bishop would help him and so might the editor of *The Jupiter*. His immediate target was the bishop who was about to make his visit to London. But the bishop was slow to see the point of Mr Slope's speculations on the dean's successor. He was taken aback when Mr Slope pointed out that he himself deserved the post and would be useful in it. The bishop promised he would do what Mr Slope said, adding that he was troubled about the hospital, which he thought should be given to Mr Quiverful. Mr Slope did not object. He looked forward to his own success, joining his hopes of the deanery to his hopes of Eleanor Bold. He wrote to two influential friends who might support him before paying his customary evening visit to the signora.

NOTES AND GLOSSARY:

***Ce n'est que le premier pas qui coûte*:** (*French*) it is only the first step that is difficult

chief commissioner of national schools: one of the schools established by the National Society founded in 1811 to promote the education of the poor

***currente calamo*:** (*Latin*) offhand, without premeditation

A great man . . . had been once much condemned for dating a letter from Windsor Castle: Thomas Babington Macaulay (1800-59), English historian and politician, wrote to his constituents in this way in 1839

Chapter 33: Mrs Proudie Victrix

During the week that followed, the dean lived on; Mr Slope received no reply from his influential friends; Mrs Bold became more and more friendly with the Stanhopes. Charlotte Stanhope had encouraged the friendship, to foster Bertie's hopes of marriage. Eleanor had not forgotten Mr Arabin's affectionate words, though she was still angry with him. But if he would acknowledge he had wronged her, she would forgive him. She knew she would meet him at the garden fête Miss Thorne had arranged at Ullathorne, to which all the notables of the county had been invited. The signora had even persuaded Miss Thorne to invite Mr Slope, whom Eleanor had avoided since her return. To her dismay she found it was planned she should go to Ullathorne in his company. By this time Dr Proudie had returned from London. Mrs Proudie felt she had shown him how agreeable she could be when he did as she suggested. She told him she had heard of Mr Slope's ambition to become dean, which she thought ridiculous. The bishop said that since she and Mr Slope did not now get on, it might be advantageous if he became dean, thus ceasing to be chaplain. Mrs Proudie made it clear that in her view Mr Slope could cease to be chaplain without becoming dean. Mr Slope, she believed, had behaved disgracefully with the signora. It was time he was shown up in his true light.

NOTES AND GLOSSARY:

Victrix: (*Latin*) feminine of 'victor'

horse-collars to be grinned through: 'The grinning-match is performed by two or more persons . . . each of them having his head thrust through a horse's collar' (Strutt, *Sports and Pastimes*, 1802)

Quintains: targets for horsemen to tilt at

that had been tried: in 1839 the Earl of Eglinton staged a tournament in his castle in Ayrshire

'albeit, unused to the melting mood': see Shakespeare's *Othello*, V. 2. 352

'Her bairn respectit like the lave': 'The Cotter's Saturday Night' by Robert Burns (1759-96), verse 8

Petruchio: the principal character in Shakespeare's *Taming of the Shrew*. He 'tamed' his wife Katherine

the new parochial universal school committee: universal primary education did not come to England until 1870

'I'll dean him': compare 'I'll Slope him', Chapter 17

Medea: in Greek legend, the princess who helped Jason to win the Golden Fleece

Robson's edition: a comic version of Medea's story was produced in 1856

Griselda: the model of wifely patience and submission, in, for example, 'The Clerk's Tale' by Geoffrey Chaucer (1345?-1400)

Chapter 34: Oxford – The Master and Tutor of Lazarus

After Eleanor left Plumstead, Mr Arabin decided he had made a fool of himself. He acknowledged he loved Eleanor, but perhaps he was too old for love. He thought that Eleanor did not care for him and decided to try to forget her. That evening he seemed the most cheerful of the party: Mr Harding was sad at Eleanor's departure; Archdeacon Grantly was preoccupied with the possibility that Mr Slope might succeed the ailing dean of Barchester. Mr Arabin and Dr Grantly discussed the contents of Mr Slope's letter to Eleanor. Mr Arabin hinted that Eleanor might not care for Mr Slope. He did not believe Mr Harding should go to see the bishop about the hospital. Mr Arabin had already persuaded Dr Grantly to write to Dr Gwynne, the master of Lazarus, about the matter. Nothing should be done until he gave his opinion. Dr Grantly was mainly concerned to defeat the schemes of Mr

Slope: he hoped that Dr Gwynne would help, but unfortunately Dr Gwynne was not anxious to interfere. Neither he nor his colleague, the Tutor of Lazarus, thought Mr Slope a suitable name for the deanery. They believed Mr Quiverful was likely to get the hospital, but in that case Mr Harding might well become the dean.

NOTES AND GLOSSARY:

Wertherian grief: *The Sorrows of Young Werther* (1774) by J.W. von Goethe (1749-1832) was a widely known account of hopeless romantic love

***malgré lui*:** (*French*) in spite of himself

***coup de main*:** (*French*) a sudden attack

***Deus ex machina*:** (*Latin*) 'The god from the machine', who often appears to settle matters at the end of Classical dramas

***dénouements*:** dénouement (*French*) is the final unravelling of a plot in a drama or novel

protection: the system of developing home industries by imposing taxes on foreign imports

credit system: the system which allowed undergraduates to run up large bills for goods which they had not paid for

alma mater: the name (*Latin*, 'benign mother') given by an undergraduate to the university or college of which he is a member

eating for the bar: student barristers are required to eat in the Hall of the Inns of Court a fixed number of times per term before being 'called' to the bar

doubles: evasive turns or shifts in the action

Chapter 35: Miss Thorne's Fête Champêtre

On the eve of the Ullathorne sports Dr Gwynne and Mr Arabin arrived in Barchester from Oxford and the bishop returned from London. Great preparations had been made at Ullathorne to provide for the requirements of the gentry and the tenants who had been invited to the sports but who could not be entertained together. Miss Thorne hoped that some of the young gentlemen would take part in her sports, but it was doubtful whether the men would care to take part in such heroic efforts or whether the ladies would be willing to do without their company. The weather was fine; the equipment for the sports had been erected. Miss Thorne could not persaude her brother to joust on horseback, but she had more hope of a young farmer, who was a favourite of hers. The country people were beginning to arrive, though her steward had some trouble keeping out intruders.

NOTES AND GLOSSARY:

Fête Champêtre: (*French*) outdoor entertainment

Directory: the executive body governing France during part of the revolutionary period (October 1795 – November 1799)

ha-ha: a trench at the end of a garden or path, which marked its boundary, without interfering with the view

***sub dio*:** (*Italian*) in the open air

***déshabilles*:** (*French*) casual dress

devilled: grilled with a hot sauce

rattletrap: any rickety or shaky thing

Chapter 36: Ullathorne Sports – Act I

The more fashionable guests were slow to arrive; there were some mishaps – physical and social. The Grantlys came with Mr Harding; Mr Arabin saw Eleanor being helped from the Stanhopes' carriage by Mr Slope; the Proudies arrived to some public attention. Miss Thorne's champion attempted to demonstrate how a target should be hit from horseback, only to be thrown from his horse. Eleanor explained privately to her father that it had been necessary to travel with Mr Slope. She thought Slope was an unpleasant man and she bitterly denounced the archdeacon for letting her father think she meant to marry him. She promised that, whatever she might do, she would tell her father first.

NOTES AND GLOSSARY:

***quid pro quo*:** (*Latin*) something given in exchange for something else

roquelaure: a cloak reaching to the knee

toxophilites: lovers of archery

Chapter 37: The Signora Neroni, the Countess De Courcy, and Mrs Proudie Meet Each Other at Ullathorne

Among the last to arrive were Signora Neroni followed by the Countess De Courcy, who tried to excuse her lateness by referring to the state of the roads. By the time her ladyship entered the house, the signora was already settled on her couch, surrounded by admirers. In passing by the signora's couch to go out on to the lawn, the countess stared at the signora who stared boldly back. The countess was not accustomed to being treated in this way. On the lawn the countess met Mrs Proudie. They gossiped about their hostess and the countess learned from Mrs Proudie that the signora was an abominable woman from Rome, who had ruined Mr Slope. Meanwhile the signora had trapped Mr Thorne and convinced him that she had been ill-used. He promised to visit her in Barchester. But his present duty was to escort Lady De Courcy to the tent where dinner was to be served. The guests paired off, Eleanor only managing to escape Mr Slope by taking Bertie Stanhope's arm. Mr Arabin was left looking after the signora in the drawing room.

NOTES AND GLOSSARY:

Leohunter: after Mrs Leo Hunter, a celebrity hunter, in *Pickwick Papers* (1836) by Charles Dickens

way-warden: a person elected to supervise the highways of a parish or district

'will gaze an eagle blind . . . Hesperides': Shakespeare, *Love's Labour's Lost*, IV. 3. 330-7

***aetat.*:** (*Latin*) aged

***nata*:** (*Latin*) born, née

Charybdis . . . Scylla: a whirlpool and a sea monster between which Odysseus, the hero of Homer's *Odyssey*, had to steer

Chapter 38: The Bishop Breakfasts and the Dean Dies

As the guests sat down, the dean of Barchester died, but the news did not arrive until the feast was over. Everyone seemed cheerful except Mr Arabin. He felt his new parsonage needed a wife. He did not mind Eleanor liking Mr Slope, but she had refused to tell him whether their relationship was any more serious. That morning he had seen Mr Slope help Eleanor out of the carriage they had arrived in. In a melancholy frame of mind, Mr Arabin was trapped by the signora who knew his feelings for Eleanor. Mr Arabin was a more formidable prey than Mr Slope (of whom she was tired) or Mr Thorne (who might be useful to her). He was a gentleman of intelligence and character. He thought the signora beautiful and charming, well able to soothe him in his present mood. She reproached him for his dullness – the party, after all, was being given in his honour. She compared him unfavourably with Mr Slope: Mr Arabin's shyness would fail to bring him success, while Mr Slope's self-assertion would bring him the good things of life Mr Arabin pretended to despise. At that moment Eleanor looked out of the dining room to see where Mr Arabin was, and the signora caught her in the act. The signora was willing to help Mr Arabin to gain Mrs Bold's affection, if Mr Arabin would confide in her. He told her he admired Mrs Bold and would like to marry her. She extracted from him the confession that he thought the signora the more beautiful of the two, and sent him to fetch some food from the dining room. When he had done so, Miss Thorne begged him to come to the table, persuading Bertie Stanhope to give up his place. So Mr Arabin sat down on one side of Eleanor, while Mr Slope sat on the other, and Bertie stood behind, meditating a proposal of marriage. For the first time, the two rival clergymen were introduced. Left on her own, Signora Neroni marvelled once again how easy it was to get men to do what she wanted. Mr Arabin's openness was something new in her experience. If Bertie failed with Eleanor Bold, she might consider helping Mr Arabin.

NOTES AND GLOSSARY:

'Twas merry in the hall when the beards wagged all': from *Five Hundred Points of Good Husbandry* by Thomas Tusser (1524?-80)

Gordian knots: the Gordian knot was an ingeniously tied knot which Alexander the Great severed with his sword

begging the question: making an assumption about the issue under discussion

you own the impeachment: you admit the charge (of being in love)

'His bishoprick let another take': a quotation from Acts, 1:20

***malgré lui*:** (*French*) in spite of himself

Chapter 39: The Lookalofts and the Greenacres

The arrangements for the entertainment of the lower orders at Ullathorne had also been successful, though Harry Greenacre's fall had been a set-back. More serious was the attempt of the Lookalofts to cross the division that separated the gentlefolks from the tenants. Mrs Lookaloft had led her daughters boldly into Miss Thorne's drawing-room very much to the disgust of her neighbour, Mrs Greenacre, whose husband was just as substantial a tenant as Mr Lookaloft. The Greenacres took pleasure in criticising the inappropriateness of Mrs Lookaloft's dress and in recounting Miss Thorne's frigid reception of them. Farmer Greenacre was content with his position in life: nothing the Lookalofts could do would cause him any sorrow. Miss Thorne's steward kept intruders from Barchester away from the feast though Farmer Greenacre urged him to be generous. In the marquee the gentry drank the health of Lord De Courcy, who was absent, and his son made a speech in reply. In the dining-room the bishop drank the health of Miss Thorne.

NOTES AND GLOSSARY:

'Friend, thou has come up hither to high places . . . ': see Luke, 14: 8-10

elysium: paradise

a Barchester Pandemonium . . . nectar . . . ambrosia . . . fields of asphodel: it was dreadful to be separated from his girl-friend and sent back with the damned to Barchester when good food and drink were about to be distributed to the blessed in Ullathorne

Cerberus: the three-headed monster who traditionally guarded the Underworld

the unjust steward: see Luke 16:1-10

a competing examination before the civil service commissioners: competitive examinations for the Civil Service were introduced in 1855

Chapter 40: Ullathorne Sports – Act II

Mr Slope had drunk enough champagne to feel able to propose to Eleanor. He followed her out on to the lawn; she tried to repel him. He thought she was angry with him because he had not proposed sooner. He insisted on walking with her, since he had something to say. She seemed to be less welcoming than she ought to have been. He poured out his feelings for her. He tried to put his arm round her waist. Eleanor boxed his ears and ran away, saying she would never speak to him again. Mr Slope vowed revenge. He had made a mistake in allowing himself to be tempted by ways of life beneath his own standards. Now he would rise beyond the place where he had stumbled and denounce its snares to the world. He went back to the group of clergy where the bishop was talking to Dr Gwynne. The bishop introduced him as his 'present chaplain' but Mr Slope did not mind. He had received an encouraging note from the editor of *The Jupiter* about his candidacy for the position of dean. At that moment a servant arrived to announce that the dean was dead. Mr Slope lost no time in returning to Barchester. Eleanor, meanwhile, had gone back towards the house in tears.

NOTES AND GLOSSARY:

'That which has made them drunk . . . ': see Shakespeare, *Macbeth*, II.2.1

Bacchus: the god of wine in Roman mythology

From such a sharp and waspish word as 'no'/To pluck the sting: from *Philip Van Artevelde* by Henry Taylor

Belgravia: a fashionable district in London

the low-heeled buskin of modern fiction: the shoes worn by tragic actors were high-heeled. Fiction, Trollope implies, cannot deal adequately with tragic emotions

Agamemnon's face: by a mistake Agamemnon found he had sworn to sacrifice his daughter, Iphigenia, in return for a favourable wind

the god . . . abstained from mouthing empty threats: Neptune, in Virgil's *Aeneid*, Book 1
Baal: a heathen god in the Old Testament

Chapter 41: Mrs Bold Confides her Sorrow to her Friend Miss Stanhope

When Eleanor reached the lawn, she wondered what to do. She wanted to avoid Mr Slope. She saw Charlotte Stanhope and went to join her. She was so upset that she told Charlotte what had happened. Charlotte shrouded her inward delight in sympathy. This was Bertie's opportunity. With Mr Slope out of the way he might be induced to ask Eleanor to marry him. Charlotte suggested Bertie would escort Eleanor back to Barchester. They looked for Bertie in the drawing room but found only Mr Arabin still under the spell of the signora. He rose to make awkward conversation with Eleanor. She told him she was returning to Barchester, but they were too shy to speak frankly to one another. The ladies resumed their search for Bertie.

NOTES AND GLOSSARY:

Pegasus: a winged horse associated with poetry
be-sirened: attended by a siren (one of those who tried to entice Odysseus to his death)
Mount Ida: the scene of the judgement of Paris (see note on Chapter 5). The offspring of Venus who was one of the three contestants, was Aeneas
Damon and Phillis: classical names for shepherd and shepherdess

Chapter 42: Ullathorne Sports – Act III

Charlotte and Eleanor discovered Bertie in the garden. Much to Eleanor's embarrassment, Charlotte told him what had happened. Charlotte left Eleanor with Bertie, who now proceeded to do his duty. Although he found Eleanor agreeable, he had no desire to settle down in Barchester. But had promised his sister to ask Eleanor to marry him. After some talk about his future plans, he explained how anxious Charlotte was to see him settled in life. He only wanted her to let his sister believe that he had proposed and she had declined. Eleanor was extremely angry. She thought she should find her own way home. But Bertie persuaded her that this would embarrass him. She found it difficult to be angry for long with Bertie: he was too good-natured and unaffected. She went back to Barchester in Dr Stanhope's carriage and Bertie went home on foot.

NOTES AND GLOSSARY:

***désoeuvré*:** (*French*) idle

***preux chevalier*:** (*French*) gallant knight
Mormonism: polygamy was part of the practice of the Church of the Latter Day Saints up to 1890
Dannecker: Johann Heinrich von Dannecker (1758-1841), German sculptor
exordium: (originally *Latin*) prologue, introduction
'*tuum*' . . . '*meum*': (*Latin*) 'what is yours' . . . 'what is mine'

Chapter 43: Mr and Mrs Quiverful are made Happy. Mr Slope is Encouraged by the Press

Before she left for Ullathorne, Mrs Proudie and the bishop had written to Mr and Mrs Quiverful asking them to call at the bishop's palace. There was much excitement at Puddingdale: it seemed that Mr Quiverful was to get the hospital after all. Now it would be possible to pay the grocer's bill. The Quiverfuls' visit to Barchester was a success: everyone began to think about moving house. The next visitor at the palace was Dr Gwynne who had promised to see the bishop about the Hospital. Mrs Proudie, who stood her ground in the bishop's study, told him the appointment had been given to Mr Quiverful. Dr Gwynne took his leave. Elsewhere Mr Slope was enjoying a leading article in *The Jupiter* which congratulated Barchester on the new arrangements for the Hospital. It went on to suggest that Mr Slope was a suitable person to become dean. He was still rather humiliated by Eleanor's rejection of him, and he could not quite free himself from thinking of the signora.

NOTES AND GLOSSARY:
***Little Dorrit*:** *Little Dorrit*, by Charles Dickens, appeared in monthly numbers from December 1855 to June 1857
***detur digniori's*:** (*Latin*) let it be given to the worthier
Mr Longman: the publisher of *Barchester Towers*, whose reader had tried to persuade Trollope to reduce his novel to two volumes
unregenerated vipers: see Matthew 3:7
'Suffer little children, and forbid them not': see Matthew 19:14
'Take heed that ye despise not . . . ': Luke 17:2-3
That comes of the reform bill: the bishops had been much criticised for voting against the Reform Bill when it was first presented in the House of Lords in 1831
the Greek play bishops: reference unknown
redivivus: (*Latin*) revived
no talk of a new American president: a new American President, James Buchanan, took office in 1857

Chapter 44: Mrs Bold at Home

When Eleanor reached home, she found Mary, her sister-in-law, there. It was not easy to tell her what had happened since she had never favoured Eleanor's friendship with the Stanhopes and Mr Slope. Mary tried to comfort her and at least she had the consolation of her son's affection. The next day she told her father. He was not surprised at Mr Slope's conduct but he urged her to tell the Grantlys. Eleanor commiserated with her father on his loss of the Hospital, but Mr Harding had no complaint. She tried to persuade him to come and live with her, but he preferred to keep his lodgings in the High Street. A note from the signora invited Eleanor to visit her and announced Bertie's departure for Italy. Eleanor promised to visit the signora next day.

NOTES AND GLOSSARY:

Mentor: in Greek mythology, he was an old Ithacan, a friend of the hero Odysseus, a wise and faithful counsellor

Job's comforter: someone who in offering comfort adds to the sorrow of the sufferer by suggesting he brought it on himself

***pied à terre*:** (*French*) a temporary or secondary lodging

Chapter 45: The Stanhopes at Home

When Charlotte and the signora got back from Ullathorne, they waited eagerly for Bertie's return, but when he walked in, it was clear his efforts had come to nothing. Dr Stanhope had not been satisfied with his family's behaviour that day. He refused to maintain his son in idleness any longer, and lost no time in telling him to leave. He was persuaded to give his son an allowance, provided he went back to Italy. Next day Eleanor made her promised visit to the signora. But she had not invited Eleanor to talk about Bertie. She began to ask Eleanor about her feelings for Mr Arabin. Was it not the case that Eleanor loved him, for the signora was sure he loved her? Eleanor was astounded, but the signora answered her that Mr Arabin knew nothing of what the signora had said. She knew of his love from her own observation. She believed that if Eleanor rejected any approach he might make, he would not ask again. Eleanor felt unhappy that her feelings had been obvious to a stranger, and that Mr Arabin had revealed to the signora what he had concealed from Eleanor herself. But she could not disbelieve what the signora has said. She was sure that if Mr Arabin proposed to her, she would accept.

NOTES AND GLOSSARY:

pauls: a small papal silver coin

***insouciance*:** (*French*) indifference

***décolleté*:** (*French*) low cut

***soupçon*:** (*French*) hint

With him, yea will stand for yea, and nay for nay: see James 5:12

Chapter 46: Mr Slope's Parting Interview with the Signora

Next day the signora was surrounded by visitors. Mr Arabin came believing she would help him with his problems; Mr Slope came, dreaming of becoming dean; Mr Thorne was paying his promised visit. The signora introduced her little girl to Mr Thorne, though he was rather unsure how to deal with her. The talk turned to who was to be the new dean. The signora teased Mr Slope about his hopes and about whom he would choose to share the deanery with him. Clearly, her hints referred to Mrs Bold and Mr Arabin felt painfully embarrassed. He was ready to believe that Eleanor had accepted Slope. The signora then asked whether it was possible the lady had refused him. Her bitter taunts about his faithlessness drove Mr Slope from the house. The signora's action was obviously the revenge of a woman who had been scorned.

NOTES AND GLOSSARY:

hang up their harps on the willows: see Psalm 137:2

Ichabod: see I Samuel 4:21

Sir Charles Grandison: the hero of the novel of that name by Samuel Richardson (1689-1761); he was supposed to be the model of Christian courtesy

''Tis conscience that makes cowards of us all': see Shakespeare's *Hamlet*, III. 1.83

'It's gude to be merry and wise': see note on Chapter 27

Chapter 47: The Dean Elect

During the following week all Barchester wondered who was to be the new dean. Mr Slope seemed to be the favourite candidate and made a mysterious visit to London. The archdeacon was still agitated about the possibility of Eleanor's marriage to Mr Slope and of his becoming dean. He was not satisfied with the outcome of Dr Gwynne's visit to the bishop. Nor was he satisfied with Mr Arabin's conduct; he was dismayed to find that his name was being linked with the signora. As the Grantlys were discussing these matters one evening before dinner, they were surprised by the unexpected arrival of Mr Harding. He came to tell them he had been offered the deanery of Barchester. Dr and Mrs

Grantly were overjoyed, but Mr Harding had some doubts: he felt he was too old and unsuited to the spirit of the times. Despite Dr Grantly's protestations, he was inclined to refuse the offer.

NOTES AND GLOSSARY:

***fait accompli*:** (*French*) a scheme already carried out and irrevocable

'But me no buts': 'Don't say "but" to me'

crotchets: perverse fancies

Chapter 48: Miss Thorne shows her Talent at Match-making

Miss Thorne had decided that Mr Arabin ought to have a wife; she could think of no one better than Mrs Bold. She invited her to spend some time at Ullathorne where the match between them was soon made. When Mr Arabin went to Plumstead next morning Mrs Grantly was delighted that the misunderstanding about Eleanor was over. She seemed to forget how much she and her husband had contributed to it.

NOTES AND GLOSSARY:

petard: an engine of war, filled with gun-powder and fastened to gates, barricades etc. See *Hamlet,* III. 4:206-7

Chapter 49: The Belzebub Colt

Miss Thorne was surprised that her guests had become engaged so quickly but she was happy to congratulate Eleanor. Next morning Mr Arabin and Eleanor had to pay some attention to Mr Thorne's concern over one of his horses, but when he had gone, they were able to enjoy the assurance of one another's love. Eleanor was happy to find someone she could trust and who would support her through life. She soon returned to Barchester to tell her father. He began by telling her he had been offered the deanery but that he intended to refuse it. She gradually found it possible to say that she was engaged to Mr Arabin. He was so astonished that he could scarcely believe it. But Mr Arabin was everything Mr Harding could have wished for a son-in-law. He promised to love him as a son. It occurred to him that Mr Arabin might be the new dean.

NOTES AND GLOSSARY:

the parasite plants grow and prosper: the ancient idea that the elm is wedded to the vine it supports is beautifully expressed in *Metamorphoses*, Book xiv, 661*ff* by P. Ovidius Naso (43BC-17AD). It is also found in Milton's *Paradise Lost*, v, 215-19

Chapter 50: The Archdeacon is Satisfied with the State of Affairs

While father and daughter were talking, Dr Grantly came to explain that he now knew he had been wrong about Eleanor and Mr Slope. Eleanor left it to her father to tell Dr Grantly of her engagement. The archdeacon was astonished and ashamed. Mr Harding suggested that Mr Arabin might be the new dean. They agreed to go to London, consulting Dr Gwynne on the way. As the archdeacon went home to Plumstead, he met Mr Slope, who looked unconcerned, although he had been dismissed by the bishop that morning. As the archdeacon passed the Hospital, he called to congratulate the Quiverfuls on their good fortune. Then he met Dr Arabin and was able to congratulate him. He had quite made up his mind that Eleanor should be married at Plumstead. As Mrs Grantly said, she had more sense than they gave her credit for.

NOTES AND GLOSSARY:

***nil admirari* doctrine:** (*Latin*) to wonder at nothing; to be indifferent (from Horace, *Epistles*, i, 6, i)
Solomon: son of David and King of Israel in the tenth century BC, noted for his wisdom
***protégé*:** (*French*) one under the protection of another
***congé*:** (*French*) permission to leave, dismissal

Chapter 51: Mr Slope bids Farewell to the Palace and its Inhabitants

Since the party at Ullathorne, Mr Slope had seen little of the bishop and his wife. He was no longer the confidential servant of the palace; Mrs Proudie had beaten him. He had heard confidentially from London that he was not to be the new dean. Mr Slope wrote to a well-connected lady in London explaining he was free for work elsewhere. The bishop, meanwhile, had asked to see him. When he entered the study, Mrs Proudie was there. The bishop said he regretted he had to complain about his conduct, and in particular of his behaviour with the signora, and he suggested that Mr Slope should go back to London at once. Mrs Proudie added that if he gave up the signora, he was welcome to take up the curacy at Puddingdale. Mr Slope expressed pity for the bishop and hoped that heaven would forgive Mrs Proudie. He returned to London, where he married the well-connected lady, now widowed. There was never any further doubt about who wielded power in Barchester: the bishop never again attempted to disobey Mrs Proudie.

NOTES AND GLOSSARY:

***couleur de rose*:** (*French*) rose colour

Is second childishness, and mere oblivion . . .: see Shakespeare, *As You Like It*, II. 7.165-6

facile princeps: (*Latin*) easily the first

At last he rose and twitched his mantle blue . . .: see Milton, *Lycidas*, lines 192-3

Chapter 52: The New Dean takes Possession of the Deanery and the New Warden of the Hospital

Mr Harding and Dr Grantly went to Oxford to see Dr Gwynne about the deanery. Dr Gwynne tried to persuade Mr Harding to accept it but he was content with the suggestion that Mr Arabin should have it. They went to London where suggestions were made in the right places. Mr Arabin was appointed Dean of Barchester. Eleanor cried with sadness that her father was not to have his promotion and with joy that it was to go to her future husband. She insisted that Mr Harding should live with them at the deanery. Mr Harding then decided he should introduce Mr Quiverful to the old men at the Hospital, which he did with great friendliness and thoughtfulness. Although it was said that no one could take the place of Mr Harding, his introduction of Mr Quiverful had assured that the latter would be treated with respect.

NOTES AND GLOSSARY:

Westminster Abbey: the principal cathedral church of Westminster, a short distance from the Houses of Parliament

Bishop of Belgravia: an imaginary bishopric whose name derives from a fashionable London Square

the Marquis of Kensington Gore: another imaginary title based on a London district, which had been fashionably developed as a result of the Great Exhibition of 1851

Lord High Steward of the Pantry Board: an imaginary title modelled on the many offices (often hereditary) attached to the Royal Household

Windsor Castle: the ancient castle twenty miles from London which had been transformed in the reign of George IV into a comfortable royal residence

their state of anarchy: the time when they had been without a warden

Chapter 53: Conclusion

Eleanor and Mr Arabin were married with much rejoicing by Archdeacon Grantly, who gave presents to all his relatives with unaccustomed generosity. After a honeymoon abroad, the Arabins settled down quietly in Barchester. Mrs Proudie did not attempt to interfere with the affairs of the cathedral but confined herself to the larger problems of the diocese. The Grantlys and the Arabins were on the best of terms, though Eleanor had absorbed many of her husband's high church notions. Mr Arabin was a hard-working dean and a conscientious scholar. The Stanhopes went back to Italy. Mr Harding continued to be the simple careful clergyman he had always been. He was simple, humble, good and devout, always attempting to put into practice the precepts of his religion.

NOTES AND GLOSSARY:

Erard: Sebastian Erard (1752-1831), famous French maker of musical instruments

Exhibition: the Great Exhibition of 1851

certain very heavy ecclesiastical legal expenses: a reference to the trial in the ecclesiastical courts of G.A. Denison (1805-96) which turned on a dispute between Evangelicals and High Churchmen over a point of religious doctrine

Archbishop of Canterbury: at this time John Bird Sumner (1780-1862) who had Evangelical sympathies

Anathema maranatha: from I Corinthians 16:22; 'Anathema' means 'a curse' but 'maranatha' means 'the Lord is coming'. Since the two words occur together in the text, they were both thought to mean a curse of excommunication

Part 3

Commentary

Studying the novel

Novels are generally read simply for pleasure. Intent on what happens next, the reader may have little awareness of the way in which his interest is being held through deliberate manipulation by the novelist. Studied more closely, however, the novel is soon observed to have a plan. It may be that the novelist takes great care to conceal his design from the reader. It is part of the pleasure of many novels that they are 'just like life'. The narrative flows in a wayward, beguiling way which reminds us of the haphazardness, the unpredictability of everyday living and yet, out of an apparently random flow, patterns emerge.

Barchester Towers is not constructed in a rigidly systematic way. It consists of a number of inter-related narratives which follow the fortunes of a group of people in the cathedral city of Barchester during the summer months of a year in the middle of the nineteenth century. Since it is a sequel to *The Warden* (1855), it assumes that we have some knowledge of, and sympathy with, characters who have appeared in the earlier novel, but Trollope is careful to ensure that *Barchester Towers* has an independent life of its own. *The Warden* was a rather narrowly conceived study of the effect on a man of good conscience of a public campaign designed to prove that he was benefiting unjustly from a charity meant for others. It was a polemical novel; it attacked publicly recognisable targets such as *The Times* newspaper, the writings of Thomas Carlyle (1795-1881) and the novels of Charles Dickens. It was a highly literary novel in which parody and imitation had a prominent place. *Barchester Towers* is much broader: it has many more characters whom it treats in greater depth. Its purpose is much less easily defined; its characters are not subordinated to a single theme. It has something of the fluidity of casually recollected experience. The characters that Trollope brings together have a greater degree of freedom: Trollope allows them to be themselves. Out of what they are, out of their ambitions and interests, desires and expectations, modified by commitments already entered into, the action of the novel begins to take shape.

The life that Trollope records is that of the principal inhabitants of Barchester, clergymen of the Church of England and their wives. The life of the church in Trollope's time provided many opportunities for the novelist. Religion was one of the dominant interests of the middle-class public for which the novelists wrote. In the nineteenth century religious issues were of considerable political significance, and the internal structure of the church produced its own divisions of opinion and competing centres of authority. But clergymen are men as well as ministers. The human passion for self-aggrandisement is challenged as well as chastened by the church's call for self-denial. Vanity and the desire for power grow vigorously under a cloak of piety. Even clergymen may be moved to covet money and attractive women.

Much of *Barchester Towers* is concerned with the struggle for power: there is a contest for supremacy between Mr Slope and Mrs Proudie; Bishop Proudie has to fight for his own independence; there is the contest between the convictions of Mr Slope and Mrs Proudie, and the entrenched traditions of the clergymen of Barchester. Out of these conflicts, parties are formed; it becomes a matter of party politics who will become Warden of Hiram's Hospital. It is a matter of national politics who will become Dean of Barchester. As a young widow with money, Eleanor Bold attracts the attention of the unscrupulous Mr Slope and the feckless Bertie Stanhope, until she finds true affection in Mr Arabin. If Mr Arabin represents the forces of order and the continued upholding of goodness, the baleful beauty of Signora Neroni holds out a promise of confusion and disarray.

One task which faces the student of the novel is to consider how these stories are related to one another. Is it merely by chance that they are accommodated within the pages of one novel, or are they regulated by a more general theme which may be deduced from the novel, even if it is nowhere stated there? The management of the narrative may be one way of studying the underlying themes of the novel. But there may be other ways: the characters, for example, may be opposed and contrasted to one another in ways which display a significant pattern. The Stanhope family, for instance, who have assimilated ways of living which are not English, offer a strong contrast to the established patterns of Barchester. There may be a recurrent use of significant metaphors which constitutes a strand of meaning which adds to our understanding of the novel. There may be a considerable amount of comment by the author (or by the narrator who is his substitute in the novel) which explicitly guides the reader's response to the characters and events which are presented either dramatically in dialogue or by means of narrative. Nor should we forget that, although the scenes in dialogue are the most obviously dramatised elements, the way in which the author has ordered his material may produce effects of tension and surprise which may also be properly considered dramatic.

Each of these possible features of the structure of the novel may be worth studying in detail for the light it throws on the novel as a whole.

But each of them is in some sense an abstraction. Each of them – character, story, dialogue, pattern of imagery, event – is an inference or deduction which the reader makes from the flow of the language of the novel. Every sentence, every phrase, makes its own contribution to our understanding of that flow. To select this or that episode, this or that phrase, for special attention is rather like using the stop-button on a video-machine. For a moment one particular frame of a sequence is frozen and highlighted: we have to be careful that our selection has not been made arbitrarily and that it is truly representative of the material as a whole. Of course, in reading a novel we are not dealing with pictures or frames: we are paying attention to language.

One of the virtues of the novel as a form of literature is its amplitude. Chapter by chapter, episode by episode, we are immersed in the world the author has created for us; we experience the rhythm of the events of the novel; we come to see that there is a significance in them. The order of the episodes and their relation to one another controls our reception of the characters and affects our judgements of them. Sometimes the author brings them together for significant occasions, as Trollope does for Mrs Proudie's reception, or for the Ullathorne sports, so that we can see the broader social patterns which condition, and may well have produced, the behaviour the characters display as individuals. Sometimes he will show them acting out the roles which society has prescribed for them; sometimes he will follow them into their most private thoughts and feelings. Trollope is content to abide by the convention that the author knows everything about his characters. He can choose how to present them and just how much to let us know about them.

Barchester Towers is a social comedy. It deals with serious matters but it treats them lightly. Comedy, like any other literary form, has a range of effects peculiar to itself, but one of its many characteristics is to remain a little detached from the people whose experiences it displays for our enjoyment. If readers are allowed to know them too well, they may come to sympathise with them too completely. Comedy implies a certain restriction of our sympathies. The comic form of *Barchester Towers* should not allow us to feel sorry for Mr Slope or to feel affection for Mrs Proudie. But not all the characters are limited in this way. What are we to make of Eleanor Bold, or Mr Harding? Their 'reality' as characters seems different from that of Mr Slope or Mrs Proudie. And how are we to take the signora, or Bertie Stanhope?

The design of *Barchester Towers*

Before considering these topics in detail, however, it may be useful to attempt a bird's-eye view of the shape of the novel. *Barchester Towers* was first published in three volumes. Its first volume consisted of the first nineteen chapters, its second of the following fifteen, and the third volume contained the final nineteen chapters. In Volume One Trollope does more than introduce his characters. He begins to explore three areas of instability within the structure of social relationships of Barchester: first, the reopened question of who will be warden of Hiram's Hospital, which had been the central concern of the first novel in the Barsetshire series; second, the interesting triangle of forces composed of Mr Slope, Bishop Proudie and Mrs Proudie; third, the attraction Eleanor Bold and her money have for Mr Slope and Bertie Stanhope. Of the three, it is the first two topics which are most fully explored in the first volume of the novel. The Proudies, with Mr Slope in attendance, and the Stanhopes arrive in Barchester like successive waves of foreign invaders who threaten to alter the character of the country they enter. The Evangelicals threaten repression and the extinction of easy-going habits; the most extreme members of the Stanhope family, infidel and Italianate, threaten a demoralising laxity. Luckily, Mr Slope's attention to the signora causes the first rift in the Bishop's party. The first volume of the novel ends with the description of a moonlit walk in Barchester when Eleanor Bold seems likely to be swept into the apparently attractive Stanhope set.

Volume Two takes place for the most part at the rectory at Plumstead; it is the least comic section of the novel. Two new forces are introduced as counterweights to the disruptive invaders introduced in Volume One. Mr Arabin, an old antagonist of Mr Slope, has been tempted to move away from the orthodoxy of Barchester in the direction of the Church of Rome, but has returned, strengthened in spirit, to the Church of England, the middle way between Protestantism and Roman Catholicism. The Thornes of Ullathorne, who own the land nearest to Mr Arabin's church, are so purely English that even the Norman invaders of eight hundred years before seem interlopers to them. Trollope treats the Thornes comically; they are the humorous side of unyielding Conservatism, but it is on this ground that the final battles between the contending parties in this novel will be fought and it is with Miss Thorne's help that Eleanor Bold is won. Happy endings are reserved for the final volume. Volume Two presents painful misunderstandings between Eleanor and her brother-in-law, Dr Grantly, who mistakenly believes she is in love with Mr Slope. Mr Slope is under the spell of the signora, but sees Eleanor as a more sensible match. The painful scenes at Plumstead are balanced by scenes of comedy at Barchester, where Mrs Proudie gains a victory for herself and for the Quiverfuls, thus bringing to an end the question of who will be warden of Hiram's Hospital. But the Dean of Barchester dies, opening up the more interesting question of who will be the new dean. In the final chapter of the second volume, this question is discussed by influential people at Oxford, the centre of theological controversy and of zeal for the well-being of the Church of England. Hints thrown out here point to possible endings of the novel, though, despite his contract of frankness with the reader, it is still open to Trollope to have a surprise in store for us.

In Volume Three Trollope speaks of 'the melodrama which Eleanor was called on to perform [that] day at Ullathorne'. The first eight chapters are devoted to the Ullathorne sports against the background of which Eleanor Bold suffers the humiliation of being proposed to by Mr Slope and Bertie Stanhope. The tone of this volume, in contrast to that of Volume Two, is broadly comic. The Ullathorne sports are presided over by Mr and Miss Thorne, whose innocence and ignorance of the world are marks of their unsophisticated goodness. In contrast with the pretentious snobbery of the fashionable world, the old-fashioned virtues of the Thornes seem comic. Miss Thorne has arranged the sports at Ullathorne as if they were a mock medieval tournament. Trollope treats the contest between Mr Slope, Mr Stanhope and Mr Arabin for the hand of Eleanor Bold almost as if it was one of the side-shows of the event. Certainly the joke is at the expense of the suitors, but it is rather difficult for the reader not to feel that Eleanor, as cause of this absurd perturbation among the men who admire her, does not suffer in reputation from their pursuit. The ardour of Mr Slope is as ludicrous as the half-proposal Bertie Stanhope makes to take Eleanor's money to pay his debts. After the sports are over, Trollope quickly disposes of the question of who is to be warden of Hiram's Hospital. The Quiverfuls are appointed: Mrs Proudie has won. The scene is set for the resolution of the two questions that are left – who is to be Dean of Barchester, and who is to marry Eleanor Bold. With the elimination of Mr Slope and Bertie Stanhope, the latter question is reduced to 'How are Eleanor and Mr Arabin to be brought together?' Trollope lingers to extract some fun from the dashing of Mr Slope's hopes of preferment, but the ending of the novel contains only the surprise of Mr Harding's being offered the post of Dean of Barchester. Trollope's way of ending his novel is leisurely and perhaps a little self-indulgent. He enjoys teasing the reader as he brings his fiction to a close. The signora has a part to play in convincing Eleanor that Mr Arabin loves her; Miss Thorne brings the lovers together; Mr Harding gives up the offer of the deanery to his prospective son-in-law. Mr Slope leaves Barchester after a satisfying clash with Mrs Proudie; and the Quiverfuls are initiated into their new duties with the blessing of the former warden. It is a warm, prolonged happy ending, made up of the 'sweetmeats and sugar-plums' that Trollope pretends to deplore.

The structure of the novel in detail

Not all modern editions of *Barchester Towers* retain the original structure of the three-volume novel. Some print the chapters consecutively without any further division into volumes. Some divide the novel in two sections. In *Barchester Towers* Trollope weaves a number of narratives together: any attempt to group the chapters into separate units is bound to be artificial, since Trollope moves at will from story to story, sometimes following two or more of his themes within one chapter. He occasionally departs from a chronological ordering of his tale, a sign perhaps of clumsiness rather than subtlety in keeping the strands of his narrative together. Perhaps the reader will find it helpful to consider the action of the novel in eight sections, subdividing the original three-volume structure as follows: Volume One – Sections 1-2; Volume Two – Sections 3-6; Volume Three – Sections 7-8.

Section One: War in Barchester (Chapters 1-11)

Chapters 1 and 2 set the scene for the novel: the death of the old bishop puts the future of Barchester in some doubt. The clergy make up such an influential part of the community that a change in their composition means that the stability of the whole is in danger. At the very least, the death of the bishop means that his son, who has wielded so much of his father's power, may see his influence diminshed. At the same time, a new act of Parliament has been brought into force for the regulation of Hiram's Hospital: will Mr Harding, the former warden, be reappointed to the post? Chapter 3 introduces the Proudies and explains the difference between the attitudes of the new bishop and his wife and those of the previous incumbent. It appears that Barchester is now to be subject to some of the forces of change in religious spirit which have been operating in London and have been favoured by the Government. A complicating factor is that the bishop's wife is accustomed to rule her husband and to interfere in the affairs of the diocese. Chapter 4 introduces us to Mr Slope, the bishop's chaplain, and we become aware of some of the tensions and conflicts which will shape the action of the novel. The crucial passage in this chapter is that describing Mr Slope's thoughts during his train journey to Barchester in the company of the bishop and his wife. Indeed, it might be said that this reverie of Mr Slope's holds the key to the nature of the first volume of the novel: the stories of Mr Harding's return to the hospital, and of Mr Slope's flirtation with the signora and his wooing of Eleanor Bold are subordinated to the struggle between Mr Slope and Mrs Proudie, and yet 'subordinated' is scarcely the correct word. Mr Harding's hopes for a return to the Hospital and Mr Slope's love affairs are part of the story of his struggle with Mrs Proudie. Trollope's intertwined stories are separate but unified, since each has a bearing on the internal struggle for mastery which takes place in the palace of the bishop.

A closer look at the passage mentioned above tells us something about how Trollope tells his story. The narrative has a certain character of its own, a tone of voice which guides the judgement of its readers. The first paragraph (beginning 'Mr Slope soon comforted himself . . . ') is written in a neutral tone. It tells us what Mr Slope is thinking as he makes his journey, but the narration also helps us to assess the judgements he makes. Mr Slope 'knew well enough', he 'understood correctly enough', he 'rightly guessed' what kind of aims the bishop would have. Each of these comments appears to be made by the narrator, who at this point in the novel is so impersonal that the reader is only just aware of the slight pressure of his guidance. The repetition of those commendatory adverbs may be the narrator's judgement of Mr Slope: they may equally be the self-congratulatory opinions of Mr Slope himself.

In the next paragraph it is clear that the guiding voice of the narrator has become that of Mr Slope. 'He, therefore, he' has been replaced by 'Mr Slope' and projects the echo of Mr Slope's silent but insistent inner voice which repeats the pronoun which comes most easily to his mind, accompanied by the gratifying sound of his own name. Instead of rendering this internal monologue in the first person, Trollope transforms it into the third, but the narrative is undoubtedly a rendering of Mr Slope's thinking and the narrator's confirming judgement, arguably present in the first paragraph, has been withdrawn. Now Mr Slope's calculations and hypotheses have no external support. Without the narrator's guidance, the reader must judge the language for himself. If Mr Slope thinks that Mrs Proudie is 'another great mind', is the reader to suppose that Mr Slope's mind is great too? With that phrase we may have moved back to the point of view of the detached ironical narrator. If, on the other hand, it is an evaluation of himself that Mr Slope shares, the reader is not compelled to accept his opinion. Mr Slope reveals that he is avid for power, that he means to fight for what he wants, and that he is perfectly willing to use any means, however subservient, to gain his ends. He is supremely self-confident, as the final sentence reveals: four swift manoeuvres will separate the bishop from his wife, transform the bishop's character, defeat Mrs Proudie and set the bishop free. The simplicity of the grammatical pattern here mirrors the simplicity of Mr Slope's thinking: each of the verbs describes some strikingly effective action, the agent of which is Mr Slope himself. There can be no doubt about the boldness of Mr Slope's fantasy nor of its immaturity. We are being allowed to hear the internal boasting of a self-infatuated young man.

But the narrator makes doubly sure that the reader will not miss what has been implied. In the paragraph that follows Trollope is offering us a picture of a man who is collected, ruthless, and ambitious, without any sense of limitations of his position. He may be evil and dangerous, or (since *Barchester Towers* is a comedy) he may simply be a fool. But the narrator makes it quite clear that he dislikes Mr Slope – he tells us explicitly that he can hardly bear to shake him by the hand. One sentence in particular offers a clear view of what is wrong with Mr Slope's outlook on life: 'Let him be supreme who can.' The self-assertion which that sentence implies reminds us of very much more substantial literary villains than Mr Slope – of Iago, perhaps, in Shakespeare's *Othello*, or of Edmund in his *King Lear*, or of Satan in *Paradise Lost* by John Milton (1608-74). Here is a man who recognises no authority and whose goal is absolute power over the minds of his followers. But the references to the Queen's supremacy, and to Mr Slope's indifference to consecration and ordination, which precede this brief sentence, suggest that he is dangerously subversive of the established order of the Church of England. In the royal declaration prefaced to the Thirty-Nine Articles agreed on by the whole clergy in 1562 ('For the avoiding of diversities of opinions and for the establishing of consent tending true religion'), the King, Henry VIII, had clearly reminded his subjects that he was the 'Supreme Governor of the Church, within these Our Dominions'.

Mr Slope's hatred of royal authority, and of the traditions of the church which only recognised as priests those who had been lawfully admitted to the priesthood, shows that he is willing to disregard customs of the Church of England which had been established for centuries. In being willing to do this, Mr Slope, however unwittingly, constitutes a threat to the right conduct of the State itself. In loathing such absolute individualism, Trollope is following the central tradition of English political thinking: he prefers the established order of things, and the system of authority which exists, to any self-appointed dictatorship.

Chapter 4 has a structural significance much greater than any that has gone before it. The arrival of the Proudies implies a challenge to the old order, but it is a challenge by a duly constituted authority, though it is sadly true that the bishop does not have the strength of character to exercise the authority he has been given, and the bishop's wife is too prone to believe that her rights as a wife entitle her to share it. But they bring with them a man who recognises no law but that his will shall be done. He has no authority himself, but he does not recognise the authority vested in others. Thus the scene is set for the action of the novel. A new liberal order – liberal in politics and in church affairs – will clash with the order which has existed undisturbed for many years. But the challengers carry with them the seeds of their own destruction. The bishop is weak, and he is hen-pecked. Mrs Proudie takes too much on herself. Mr Slope is Mrs Proudie's protégé: yet on the way to Barchester he is plotting against her.

In Chapter 5 the ordinary course of the narrative is resumed and it soon becomes clear that there is a state of open war between the Proudie faction and the clergymen of Barchester. In Chapter 8 Mr Harding begins to have expectations that he may be allowed to resume his former post as Warden of Hiram's Hospital. In Chapter 9, as a result of the bishop's wish that clergymen who have ceased to reside in the diocese should return to Barchester, the Stanhopes are introduced as a further source of change working within the society of the town. As a family, they have little to contribute to the religious life of Barchester. Dr Stanhope has been content to live on the income brought to him by his clerical appointments but has had no interest in his duties as a clergyman. His family are intelligent chatterers, interested in anything and committed to nothing but their own material well-being. Their rootless aestheticism, which is utterly opposed to Evangelic fervour, is no less unsympathetic to the traditional pieties of Barchester.

The two chapters (10 and 11) in which Mrs Proudie's reception is described are among the funniest in the novel. The behaviour of the signora and of Bertie Stanhope runs completely counter to the conventions of Barchester. Their clothes are minutely described: her dress of white velvet trimmed with lace and pearls is set off by a 'band of red velvet, on the centre of which shone a magnificent Cupid in mosaic, the tints of whose wings were of the most lovely azure, and the colours of his chubby cheeks the clearest pink'. Bertie 'was dressed in light blue from head to foot. He had on the loosest possible blue coat, cut square like a shooting-coat and very short. It was lined with silk of azure blue. He had on a blue satin waitcoat, a blue neck-handkerchief which was fastened beneath his coat with a coral ring, and very loose blue trousers which almost concealed his feet'. This is the stuff of comic fiction. These brilliantly inappropriate garments are meant to offer the strongest possible contrast to the sober black of the rest of the company. No other lady's dress is described: Mrs Proudie's magnificence is mentioned only when it has been destroyed by the sofa which, accidentally propelled into the middle of the room, tears off, as if symbolically, the lace train of her dress. Bertie's impertinently offhand remarks ('you are changed about sometimes, a'nt you?' and 'By the by, do you know much about the Jews?') have an unnerving effect on the bishop, while the signora speaks the language of pure melodrama.

There is a complex undercurrent to the comedy. It is ludicrous that the signora should expect the descendant of Roman emperors – even if it were at all plausible that her daughter was 'the last of the Neros' – to be blessed by a Christian bishop. But Bishop Proudie is moved to speak nicely to the signora because she is an attractive woman, though he attempts to rationalise his feelings and her language into a prosaic request that he should confirm the little girl. Nothing could be further from the truth. The signora's language hints at the significance of this meeting between her daughter and the bishop, as if it were a meeting between representatives of the old world of paganism and the new world of Christianity. In fact the meeting never takes place. The meeting which does take place in Chapter 46 between the little girl and Mr Thorne may be regarded as a substitute for it. In fact, it is a fiasco: the last of the Neros turns out to be a precocious, over-dressed little girl whose response to Mr Thorne's attentions is 'Let me go, you naughty old man, you.'

The Stanhopes offer a threat to stolid, ceremonious, ethical, unostentatious Barchester, bringing to it an unfamiliar air of dilettantism, aestheticism and a lightly veiled eroticism. Their indolence and indifference seem to offer a greater challenge than the enthusiasm of Mr Slope. They combine the acceptable and the unacceptable in a disconcerting way: they are well-connected, and have impeccable social standing, but they are artistic, improvident and disturbingly unconventional. Trollope does not allow the Stanhopes to have much effect in Barchester: similar characters in novels written later in the century would represent everything that seemed most attractive to those who wanted to escape from the conventionality of English middle-class life. (Think of what Italy is made to represent in the early novels of E.M. Forster (1879-1970) or in some of the novels of D.H. Lawrence (1885-1930)). The signora is a bed-ridden Venus, too alluring to be ignored, but only interested in playing with the men she so easily attracts. But while she is an affront to Mrs Proudie, she is no serious rival to Eleanor Bold. The masculine vigour she arouses in Mr Slope or Mr Arabin is only enough to prompt them to look elsewhere for a mate. She makes her public début at Mrs Proudie's reception to which Trollope has invited everyone who matters in Barchester. The attention Mr Slope pays her on that evening marks the first rift between Mrs Proudie and himself.

Section Two: The Return to the Hospital; the Wooing of Eleanor Bold (Chapters 12-19)

By Chapter 12 most of Trollope's cast has been assembled, though one or two of its significant figures – in particular, Mr Arabin – are reserved for later appearance. In the second section of the narrative Mr Slope's attempt to impose himself on Barchester begins. The bishop entrusts him with the task of discussing the new arrangements for Hiram's Hospital with Mr Harding and he begins by asking Mr Harding to undertake new duties. The hospital is no longer to be regarded as a sinecure. Once again the tone of the narrative suggests that the contest between the values of Mr Slope and Mr Harding is a serious one: ' "You must be aware, Mr Harding, that things are a good deal changed in Barchester," said Mr Slope. ". . . New men, Mr Harding, are now needed and are now forthcoming in the church, as well as in other professions." '

Trollope is not kind to Mr Slope. Notice how he allows Mr Harding to fill out the description of the 'new men' in question by the adjectives 'busy, uncharitable, self-lauding'. If they are more active, they have abandoned some of the essential Christian virtues which were practised by the men of former generations, notably charity and humility. The narrator is careful to stress Mr Harding's own natural goodness: he does not readily feel hostile to others; he has no high opinion of himself. Mr Slope's oblique comparison between the 'new men' of Barchester – including, of course, himself – and the new prime minister jars against our sense of the appropriate. His contempt for tradition and history implies a self-assurance, a certainty about his own rightness of judgment, which seems immodest in the younger man: it is far from obvious, as his tone implies, that he is Mr Harding's superior. On the contrary, though Trollope nowhere explicitly says so, Mr Harding is the only character in the novel whose actions are guided by a profound sense of Christian values. It is in comparison with him that Trollope means us to judge the moral worth of the other characters in the novel.

Mr Slope sees Mr Harding as nothing more than a manipulable object. He has also decided that Mr Harding's daughter, Eleanor Bold, will be a useful means of influencing her father. With her, he is more unctuous, more ingratiating. He seeks her as an ally, and Eleanor has no reason to doubt his sincerity. Only her sister, Archdeacon Grantly's wife, suspects that Mr Slope might be interested in making Eleanor his wife. It is at this point (Chapter 14) that Trollope first mentions a character who is to play a major part in the action of his novel. Mr Arabin, Fellow of an Oxford College, has been persuaded to accept the parish of St Ewold, and Dr Grantly believes he will assist him in repelling the liberalism of Bishop Proudie and the personal ambitions of Mr Slope. Trollope tells us that Mr Slope and Mr Arabin have already taken issue with one another on a theological subject. The point of the debate between them had turned on the question of authority and tradition. Mr Arabin's personal belief that a clergyman could not be clergyman at all without belonging to a tradition leading back to the church of earliest times is in sharp contrast to Mr Slope's view that what is necessary is the inner sense of conviction of the self-righteous man. Tradition and the collective wisdom of the community are set in opposition to the will of the individual. As a matter of historical fact, the doctrine of the apostolical succession was an essential aspect of the Oxford Movement's picture of the history of the Church of England. But Mr Arabin's argument is an explicit rationalisation of the reverence for the past we have already seen displayed by Mr Harding.

Although such matters of principle are to be found at the deepest level of *Barchester Towers*, the main concern of its first volume (Sections One and Two in our division) is Mr Slope's intrigue over the wardenship of the hospital. Finding that Mr Harding is not willing to act according to his instructions, Mr Slope attempts to have Mr Quiverful appointed. But he has no sooner allowed Mr Quiverful to believe that the wardenship will be his than he learns that Mrs Bold is a wealthy woman. He begins to wonder why he should not have her wealth for himself and whether it would not help his plan if his future father-in-law were well-provided for. Mr Slope is beginning to learn from experience that external events do not always conform to the shaping of his imagination, but he has not yet abandoned the attempt to force them to his will. If his altered plans no longer fit the train of events he has begun, then events must be brought in line with his intentions. This time, however, they have acquired a momentum of their own and are not so easily harnessed.

When the bishop reminds him that Mrs Proudie has already made arrangements about the hospital with Mr Quiverful, Mr Slope plays on the bishop's desire to be master in his own house, suggesting the undesirability of female interference in the affairs of the diocese. Now (in Chapter 16) Trollope reveals a weakness in Mr Slope's strategy. In supporting the claims of Mr Harding (and in playing on the bishop's wish to be free of his wife's domination), Mr Slope makes the mistake of believing he can now do without Mrs Proudie's patronage. In fact, unknown to Mr Slope, a new battle is about to begin for the control of the diocese. In his conversation with the bishop we see him taking the first step along the road which is to lead to his rupture with Mrs Proudie, whom he seriously underestimates as a political opponent.

This little episode displays some of the unseen cracks in the relationships within the bishop's party. It also reveals once again the serious lack of understanding which Mr Slope has of himself and his surroundings. What is perhaps principally to be noticed is the reciprocal action of Mr Slope and the bishop upon each other. From Mr Slope's point of view, the manipulative action is all his own: he does not see that the bishop means to use him in his private domestic battle with Mrs Proudie. The bishop is intelligent enough to be surprised that Mr Slope seems willing to move away from the protection of his patroness: Mr Slope does not quite realise that he has done so. 'Mrs Proudie is the best friend I have. I must always remember that.' But does he have a full awareness of how much he depends upon her support? Is it principled, or even prudent, to shift loyalties, as he appears to be doing? Can he make such a sharp distinction in this case between the loyalty owed to friendship and that demanded by professional duty? Mrs Proudie's patronage of the chaplain is not simply a personal matter: to her Mr Slope is an agent in her attempts to influence diocesan affairs.

Mr Slope's words betray his duplicity: 'I only speak, my lord, for your own comfort . . . for your own comfort and dignity in the diocese. I can have no other motive.' Here he is too insistent: the advertisement of the purity of his own motives would in itself lead the reader to doubt what he says, even if it had not already been made clear how intent he is upon power. How easily he has assumed responsibility for making suggestions about the Hospital: how lightly he dismisses the difficulty of undoing what he has done. Is it really possible for him to believe that Mrs Proudie's promises to Mrs Quiverful can be treated as mere inconveniences, which can be brushed aside? Is he aware that for the moment the initiative has passed to Dr Proudie, who is pleased to have brought his chaplain over to his side in his battle with Mrs Proudie?

What Trollope is charting here are the eddies of politics on a small scale. The affairs of the diocese of Barchester display in miniature the conflicts of character and intelligence, ambition and imagination which characterise the struggle for power in the affairs of the nation. The later Barsetshire and Palliser novels paint a wider canvas of parties and interests. But in *Barchester Towers* Trollope's attention is engaged by the same themes: he is absorbed by the unintended consequences of actions which have more significance than the agent realises. Seen from one point of view, such effects can be purely comic, as they are for the most part in this novel. Only a slight alteration in the author's tone and perspective is needed to show that sometimes they may be tragic.

In the second section the skein of events of which the action is composed soon becomes densely intertwined. The main strands of the action result from the plans and decisions of four main characters – Mr Harding, Mr Slope, Mrs Bold and Bertie Stanhope. Bertie, the feckless son of the Stanhope family, as we learn in Chapter 15, has spent a good deal of money and has no prospect of making any for himself. Eleanor Bold's fortune would be a great prize for him. His sisters are in no doubt that he must make Eleanor his wife. But at this point in the narrative our attention is fixed on the intentions of Mr

Slope. In his attempts to reverse the train of events he has set in motion, he tries to persuade Eleanor to intervene. Perhaps she could persuade her father to ask Mr Quiverful to stand down, or perhaps she could talk to the bishop about the matter herself. At the very least he wants Eleanor to believe that what he has most at heart is the welfare of her father – and of herself. Once again, Trollope is tracing the course of human misunderstanding for comic purposes, weaving together Eleanor's concern for her father and Mr Slope's desire for Eleanor in a web of cross-purposes. Trollope is keenly aware of the communication which can take place between two people just below the level of consciousness. Eleanor's conversation with Mr Slope reveals the resources which duplicity has at its command when confronted with simple truth. It also reveals something of the capacity for self-deception that innocence has when confronted with importunity.

Three separate traits are worth noticing in the dialogue between Mr Slope and Eleanor in Chapter 16. The first is the train of lies and half-truths which Mr Slope tells Eleanor. His main concern is to prevent an encounter between Mr Harding and the bishop. Just as he has misrepresented to the bishop Mr Harding's views about returning to the Hospital, so now he misrepresents to Eleanor the bishop's attitude to her father. The misunderstanding – and Mr Slope's part in creating it – might be discovered, if they met. Second, Mr Slope has no compunction about blackening the bishop's character by the tone he uses in referring to him. 'The bishop has been too rash,' he says. 'The bishop fancies that he has cause of anger against your father.' Bishop Proudie has many faults, but he is not the hasty, fanciful, uncharitable man that Mr Slope makes him out to be. Thirdly, we are aware of what might now be called the 'body language' which passes between Mr Slope and Eleanor. He, we must assume, is perfectly aware that beneath his apparent concern for Mr Harding's welfare runs a keen desire for closer contact with Eleanor herself. Her reaction to him is instinctive but unconscious, though it may be wondered whether the instinct that prompted her to draw back might not have given her some insight into the nature of his intentions.

Much of the action of the novel depends on Eleanor Bold's slowness in understanding her feelings, just as some of it depends on other people's misunderstanding of her. Trollope's reference to 'what has been said about her at Plumstead' throws out another strand of the action which will be more fully developed later. Eleanor's concern for her father, her willingness to think the best of Mr Slope, her unawareness of his intentions towards her, her unawareness of her real feelings about him and her lack of insight into how her behaviour is being interpreted by others knit together to produce the dense but essentially simple fabric of misunderstanding and surmise of which the novel is made.

Barchester Towers is a comedy about love and war. Its protagonist appears to be Obadiah Slope, an anti-hero whose attempts to secure money, power and the love of a desirable woman come to nothing. He has no understanding of the nature of love, and he underestimates the forces whose authority he challenges. He makes a mistake when he thinks he is the hero of the action: in reality, he is merely a tool, temporarily useful in the hands of others. The exploits of Mr Slope in the public arena are repeated in the domestic life of the bishop of Barchester. Dr Proudie's warfare is directed against his own wife, and Trollope finds much comedy in the mixed feelings of fear, resentment and dependence which the bishop has for Mrs Proudie. The bishop's first skirmish with her (in Chapter 17) is treated in a broadly comic way. After the first check of the bishop's attack, Trollope uses an inflated and exaggerated language which is intended as a mock-encouragement: 'Now, bishop, look well to thyself, and call up all the manhood that is in thee . . .'

This language mocks the bishop, even as it pretends to encourage him. It is intended to remind the reader of the high style appropriate to epic, and the old-fashioned syntax ('thyself', 'thou art', 'hast') and the repeated exhortations, which urge the bishop to act, mimic the habits of the epic poet. But the mimicry is ironic: in this battle the bishop is not a hero but a pigmy. 'After all the apron is thine own' – but which apron? Is it the garment he wears as the symbol of his ecclesiastical office – or is it the garment that might be worn more appropriately in the kitchen or the nursery? The first round of this battle is decisively won by Mrs Proudie, and Mr Slope finds, when he returns to the palace, that he has exposed himself to her attack. In her view he has erred in two ways – in paying too much attention to Signora Neroni, and in being inclined to take too much authority on himself. At the end of the first volume of the novel Mrs Proudie has taken the measure of Mr Slope: she has detected his fondness for women and his love of power: she does not approve of what she has seen.

Just as Mrs Proudie associates Mr Slope with the signora, Dr Grantly associates him with Eleanor Bold. The archdeacon does not care for the idea that his sister-in-law might be interested in the bishop's chaplain. He easily interprets her tolerance of Mr Slope's diocesan activities as approval of the man himself. Dr Grantly thinks that Eleanor might marry Mr Slope. The idea was first suggested to him by his wife, and he has not hesitated to make the suggestion to Mr Harding. Thus Trollope sets up a new misunderstanding which will run its course during the novel. Dr Grantly's capacity for rapidly imagining a possible sequence of future events is fully equal to Mr Slope's. In a moment he sees that Mr Slope 'thinks to buy the daughter by providing for the father'. Mr Harding's immediate response is that he will give up any claim to the Hospital, but Dr Grantly does not mean to be beaten. He intends Mr Harding to have the Hospital without Mr Slope's help. In the meantime Eleanor is to be invited to Plumstead out of the way of Mr Slope's attentions.

Before changing his scene to Plumstead, Trollope inserts a chapter which brings together Eleanor Bold and her two suitors, Bertie Stanhope and Mr Slope. It is evident that Slope is jealous of Bertie, and he is afraid that the signora's fondness for him will have compromised him in Eleanor's eyes. The moonlight stroll which Charlotte Stanhope devises for Bertie and Eleanor leads them past the Hospital. Mr Slope – guiltily, perhaps – wishes to hurry past, but Eleanor lingers with intense longing for her father's return to his old post. Bertie Stanhope makes himself agreeable to Eleanor, but it is obvious that his heart is not in the love-match which his sisters want him to make. As early as Chapter 15, Trollope has told us that he has no intention of allowing Eleanor to marry either Mr Slope or Bertie Stanhope, but on this occasion they both see her home. If the reader has no reason to fear that she will not marry either of those unsuitable men, it is not at all clear what Eleanor feels about them or what her intentions are. She is only beginning to recognise Mr Slope's duplicity, and she feels warmly towards the Stanhope family. The reader knows far more about the Stanhopes than Eleanor does, and Trollope keeps us guessing about how these affairs of the heart will turn out. Despite Trollope's assertion (in Chapter 15) that 'our doctrine is, that the author and the reader should move along together in full confidence with each other', a modest degree of suspense is part of the pleasure of this novel.

Section Three: Plumstead, Mr Arabin and the Thornes of Ullathorne
(Chapter 20-3)

In Chapter 20 Trollope moves to Plumstead, the parish of Archdeacon Grantly. Eleanor and her father have been invited to stay and so has Mr Arabin, who is to take up his post as a vicar of St Ewold's, a church just outside Barchester. As an upholder of the spiritual authority of the Church of England, Mr Arabin complements Dr Grantly's much more worldly concern for the temporal well-being of the church. Both are on the same side politically, but whereas Dr Grantly's conservatism is based on an allegiance to the values of a social class, Mr Arabin's loyalty is to a principle. Like many young men of the time he had been influenced by the Oxford Movement. He had sought a strict faith which would satisfy his mind as well as his spirit, and for a time he believed he might join the Roman Catholic Church. But he had remained a member of the Church of England and now attempted to reconcile a life of faith with the practical demands of the everyday world.

Trollope's presentation of Mr Arabin is grave and sympathetic. Mr Arabin as a young man was idealistic: in the term popular in the eighteenth century he had been 'enthusiastic'; a twentieth-century equivalent might be 'committed'. Now, in middle age, he realises how much he has been willing to give up for the spiritual intensity which has possessed him. Among the things he regrets is the lack of a wife and family, since as the Fellow of an Oxford college he was not permitted to marry. The tone of the 'narrative voice' here is quite different from the one in which Trollope urged Bishop Proudie to resist his wife. Trollope does not admire excessive virtue; it is a mistake, in his view, to try to be better than one's neighbour. But Mr Arabin is treated with great sympathy: he has been over-ambitious, but not dishonourable. It is to his credit that he does not allow the melancholy of these inner reflections to spoil his urbanity. Eleanor is pleased to find him good-humoured and modest in company, and she admires his spiritual seriousness. The conversation which Eleanor and Mr Arabin have in Chapter 21, when they visit Mr Arabin's new parsonage, surprises her by its 'quiet earnestness'. Eleanor is not a religious woman in any strong sense of the word, but she has the example of her father whom 'she classed . . . in her own mind apart from all others'. She has suffered bereavement and has shared in her father's trials of conscience. She does not have the brisk, practical common sense of her sister, nor the rather insensitive complacency that goes with it. There is some quality of mind and character in her which responds to Mr Arabin, although much more has to happen before it is recognised between them that they are in love.

The introduction (in Chapter 22) of Mr Wilfred Thorne of Ullathorne and his sister is a rich new source of material for Trollope. Ullathorne Hall has a considerable significance in the novel since it is at the sports which Miss Thorne organises there that its climax takes place. One might say that it is appropriate that the candidates for Eleanor Bold's hand should be finally tested at Ullathorne, which seems to represent enduring values of the English traditions. But it may equally be argued that the themes introduced by the Thornes are not developed seriously by Trollope. His characterisation of Mr and Miss Thorne owes much to Sir Walter Scott, and in particular to his novel, *Ivanhoe* (1820). Like many characters in Scott's novels, they are loyal to ancient traditions which have begun to seem out of place in the nineteenth century. Their pride of ancestry, which can be traced back beyond the Norman Conquest, seems slightly comic. They are determined to be old-fashioned and to admire nothing more modern than the eighteenth century. Trollope means to take a satirical glance at the revival of the admiration for the 'Merrie England' of the Middle Ages, which had produced a fashion for Gothic architecture, for example. But in so far as their worship of times gone by reflects a spirit of simple patriotism, Trollope admires them. It is Miss Thorne's spontaneous warmth of spirit which is of most consequence for the novel: she feels sorry for the young widow, is happy to give her the advice of an old maid, and has a sharp eye for what kind of man is most likely to make her a suitable husband.

Section Four: Mr Slope at Barchester (Chapters 24-7)

Having established Mr Arabin at St Ewold's under the patronage of the Thornes, Trollope returns to Barchester and to the fortunes of Mr Slope. Before he does so, however, he makes it clear that Eleanor Bold's feelings have not been seriously engaged by any of the new men who have made an appearance in her life. She enjoys Bertie Stanhope's company, and cares enough for Mr Arabin to be slightly jealous of the fact that he finds the signora attractive. The significant new fact in her life is not that she has become attached to a new suitor but that the memory of her love for her late husband is beginning to fade. In returning to Mr Slope, Trollope reminds the reader of the events which have led up to Mr Slope's decision to challenge Mrs Proudie over her recommendation that Mr Quiverful should be given the wardenship of Hiram's Hospital. It was in Mr Slope's interest, as a suitor for the hand of Eleanor Bold, that her father should look on him favourably, and his ambition for power in the church urged him to break his dependence on Mrs Proudie. Trollope skilfully conveys the complexity of the apparently trivial matter of who should become Warden by his sharp awareness of how a simple issue may apear complex, if it is considered from a number of different points of view.

To the outside world, Mr Quiverful's adherence to Mr Slope seems contemptibly craven; only Mr Quiverful fully realises the weight of the family responsibilities which compel him to compromise himself with Mr Slope. To Mrs Quiverful, on the other hand, her husband's remaining scruples about what is due to Mr Harding seem a deplorable neglect of his family's welfare. It is Trollope's awareness of the conflicting interests of Mr Slope and Mr Quiverful which makes his presentation of their meeting (in Chapter 24) so dramatic. Part of the drama lies in the contrast between the two men: Mr Quiverful is painfully honest; Mr Slope's rhetorical skill easily breaks the inconvenient bonds of truth-telling and promise-keeping. Mr Slope begins his interview with Mr Quiverful by reminding him of their last conversation. (It may be said here that readers in search of the truth of the matter will not find it helpful to turn back to the beginning of Chapter 15 where the first conversation between Mr Quiverful and Mr Slope was reported.) Even before Mr Slope had left Mr Quiverful on that first occasion, he had begun to reconsider the wisdom of offering him the wardenship. But he had said that Mr Harding had 'positively refused' the position, and his words to Mr Quiverful had implied that the wardenship would be his.

If we return to the second conversation between Mr Slope and Mr Quiverful it is clear that Trollope adds much that was left unsaid on the first occasion. It is an excellent example of the edited version of events which for most people goes by the name of 'memory'. Much is made in the passage of 'remembering' and 'memory'. It is only when Mr Quiverful's memory of what happened diverges from Mr Slope's account of it that he speaks up for what he believes he had been promised. It was unfortunate for Mr Slope that on the very day he had spoken to Mr Quiverful at Puddingdale, Mrs Proudie had spoken to Mrs Quiverful at Barchester. Exactly the same promises which Mr Quiverful believed had been made to him had been made to Mrs Quiverful by Mrs Proudie. Trollope's point surely is that there is a limit on the ability of the powerful to tamper with the truth to suit their own ends. Truth and right action are not to be manipulated with impunity.

The duty of keeping promises is often cited by British moralists as one of the absolute moral commands that we perceive, as it were, 'naturally', but the existence of systems of patronage in Church or State might appear to weaken this duty because the privilege conferred on the recipient is given at the will of the patron. Humble people like the Quiverfuls may sometimes feel that they live in an arbitrary world where concepts of justice and right action have no force, if the powerful person in whom they trust has changed his mind. This is what Mrs Quiverful thinks Mrs Proudie has done and she goes to Barchester to throw herself on the mercy of the bishop's wife. In supporting her appeal, Mrs Proudie puts her own authority and influence to the test.

Trollope's handling of the encounter between Mrs Proudie, Mr Slope and the bishop displays his comedy at its best. Chapter 26 must be compared with Chapter 17 ('Who Shall be Cock of the Walk?') in which Mrs Proudie asserted her will over the bishop and presumed to rebuke Mr Slope about his conduct with the signora. Mrs Proudie expects to repeat her success. Indeed, she has just gained a minor victory over her husband by compelling him to refuse an invitation from the Archbishop to go to London on his own. But when she enters the room, she sees that the letter of refusal has been reopened, and the question is once more under discussion. Trollope's presentation of this scene is complex. He dramatises the conflict between Mrs Proudie and Mr Slope, making us aware of her wilfulness and of his hypocritical smoothness. Mrs Proudie's direct method of attack is mirrored in her speech which implies that no answer contrary to her wishes can be tolerated ('What is this, bishop, about Mr Quiverful?'). She even orders Mr Slope to leave the room so that she can speak to the bishop alone. At the height of her tirade, she assails Mr Slope with a hail of questions which imply that he has no right to interfere in diocesan matters, though her own right to interfere rests on her relationship to the bishop. In her questions to Mr Slope, her tone is imperious to the point of brutality ('What business have you at all with these interviews? Who desired you to go to Mr Quiverful this morning? Who commissioned you to manage this affair?'). Mr Slope is firm; his sentences in reply are wholly under his control. He addresses himself impersonally to the facts and principles of the case. He does not refer to the bishop directly and seems to be stating the irresistible consequences of possible courses of action rather than offering any opinion of his own. In contrast to Mrs Proudie's grammatically simple torrent of questions, his sentences are grammatically complex, a fact which seems to emphasise his aloof self control: ' . . . his Lordship, as I understand it, feels it to be his duty . . . '.

In using the phrase, 'as I understand it,' Mr Slope appears to be acting as the impersonal spokesman for the bishop who remains silent throughout until Mrs Proudie makes the mistake of forcing him to choose between herself and his chaplain. Trollope makes especially good use of the bishop's silence: initially, it is the silence of timidity, then of expectation. If his wife and Mr Slope clash headlong, one of them will be defeated. As a result, he will be released from the tiresome perplexity of wondering whose advice to follow. Mr Slope sees the encounter as crucial, since, if Mrs Proudie triumphs, his own influence with the bishop will be at an end. On this occasion Mr Slope appears to win a victory. When Mrs Proudie asks the bishop whether she or Mr Slope is to leave the room, the bishop is compelled to speak. And he chooses to say that Mr Slope and he are busy.

Mr Slope consolidates his victory by telling the bishop to his face what people are saying about his wife's influence over him, but Trollope makes it plain that his triumph is short-lived. Nothing can separate the bishop from his wife: there will be other opportunities for her to influence him and occasions too private for the intrusion of Mr Slope. Once again, Trollope enters into Mr Slope's way of thinking only to show its shallowness. In the chapter that follows, we see him writing a letter to Mrs Bold which contains an invitation to Mr Harding to call on the bishop, but it also contains expressions which are too personal to be acceptable to Mrs Bold's family. This letter, delivered into the hands of Dr Grantly himself, is to provide fuel for Dr Grantly's angry distrust of his sister-in-law. But before he leaves Barchester, Trollope stages an encounter between Mr Slope and the signora in which she cruelly exposes his romantic attachment to her by making it clear that she knows about his mercenary interest in Mrs Bold. Mr Slope, so suavely self-controlled in his dealings with Mrs Proudie, is helpless in the hands of the signora. Trollope endows her with a bitter insight which seems a product of her own unhappy experience of men.

In this episode the narrative is presented very much from the point of view of the signora. To some extent Trollope shows her pleasure at the sight of Mr Slope transfixed by her insight into his motives and helplessly attempting to reconcile his desires for wordly advancement and sensual satisfaction with his profession as a clergyman. She forces him to see the contradiction between his declaration of affection for her and his wish to marry Eleanor Bold. She reminds him she is a married woman. She accuses him of a superficial romantic attachment which has nothing to do with his real aims for his own success. Is he truly prepared to sacrifice these aims for, as she puts it, 'the smiles of a lame lady'? Trollope's attitude to the signora at this point in the novel is ambiguous: is she merely a teasing cynic, or does her ruthless moral realism demonstrate a valuable honesty? At any rate, Mr Slope's triumph over Mrs Proudie has been succeeded by his humiliation at the hands of the signora. Trollope leaves his fate in balance here, but there is little doubt about the outcome of Mr Slope's attempt to impose himself on Barchester: the only question for author and reader is how his downfall will come about.

Section Five: Eleanor and her Friends at Plumstead (Chapters 28-30)

As the second volume of the novel draws to a conclusion, Trollope's treatment of his material darkens. Hitherto, the misunderstandings which have arisen between the characters have given rise to situations which have been presented either comically or satirically. Now the differences between Eleanor Bold and her family result in angry feelings and painful scenes. Trollope's narrator signals the change of mood by confessing his inability to convey the impression made on Eleanor when her brother-in-law suggested that he was afraid of the possibility of her becoming Mrs Slope.

What follows is a further example of Trollope's skill in making use of the blindness of human beings for the purposes of his fiction. Alone in her room, Eleanor is a prey to fantasies which distort the reality of the state she finds herself in. Bad as it is to be misunderstood by her father and her brother-in-law, she makes things worse by imagining that Mr Arabin has played some part in spreading malicious gossip about her. These are the black fantasies of Eleanor's temporarily deranged imagination. It may be that the reader will wonder how far these misunderstandings between Eleanor and her friends arise strictly from the characters that Trollope has established. We are not likely to wonder at the archdeacon's insensitivity, and it has been made clear that Mrs Grantly is not aware of the real state of her sister's feelings. It is more difficult to believe that Mr Harding would fail to ask Eleanor directly about her attitude to Mr Slope. It is true that on a previous occasion (in Chapter 21) Eleanor has not quite understood Mr Arabin's 'raillery'. To that extent she may have some reason for thinking that he sometimes speaks in a 'jeering, sarcastic way'. But it may be argued that the demands of plot are too evident here. The reader is made too conscious of the fact that complications, which exist only to be unravelled, are being introduced in a way that undermines our belief in the relationships and feelings Trollope has caused us to imagine.

Trollope moves round his cast of characters, shifting the point of view from which the story is told. The archdeacon realises that Eleanor is angry with him, but he fails to understand why: '. . . he thought that she was . . . angry not because she was suspected of an intention to marry Mr Slope but because such an intention was imputed to her as a crime.' Trollope's narrator is, of course 'omniscient', but he is careful not to reveal how much he knows. Indeed, one might sometimes wonder if he quite plays fair. Earlier, we noticed how a later version of the interview between Mr Quiverful and Mr Slope could not be checked against the earlier, because a full account had not been given in the first place. Another example occurs in the account which Trollope gives of Mr Arabin's remarks to Dr Grantly about what he thinks Eleanor's feelings are for Mr Slope. In Chapter 28 all that passes between them is Mr Arabin's horror that Eleanor's name should be linked with Mr Slope's. By Chapter 29 Dr Grantly positively says that Mr Arabin 'agrees with me and Susan that it is quite impossible you should be received at Plumstead as Mrs Slope'. By Chapter 30, when Eleanor angrily reproves Mr Arabin for discussing such a matter with her brother-in-law, she does not allow him to express his belief that she could never be in love with a man like Mr Slope. Has Trollope played fair? The versions of the conversation between Dr Grantly and Mr Arabin differ markedly in tone according to the teller. The reader not only has no independent account of the episode; he may well wonder whether it would have been possible for the narrator, whose account of events he has learned to trust, to report such a conversation about Eleanor between these clergymen while continuing to represent consistently the character of each. But Trollope's narrative at this point is deliberately vague and disjointed. The interest of the story lies in the way in which the partial knowledge of each of the characters helps to shape the course of the action. Chapter 30 is a chapter of misunderstandings. It recounts unrealised feelings, unfulfilled impulses, defeated intentions. First, Mr Arabin wanders about his new parsonage at St Ewold's, half believing, half disbelieving that Eleanor Bold is in love with Mr Slope. Then follows the painful and embarrassing scene between Eleanor and Mr Arabin. It is painful because Trollope is exploring areas of personal feeling he has not touched before; it is embarrassing because he appears to be manipulating his characters not to build up some consistent picture of them, but to keep his novel going. Eleanor accuses Arabin of slandering her. He gives his version of the advice he gave to Dr Grantly about receiving her as the wife of Mr Slope. She accuses him of ill-will to her because of his prejudice against Mr Slope.

It is a little difficult to believe that such painful, private matters could be discussed in such tones of rancour between a woman of Eleanor's generosity of spirit and a man of Mr Arabin's principles. And Trollope is aware of the awkwardness: 'How easily would she have forgiven and forgotten the archdeacon's suspicions had she but heard the whole truth from Mr Arabin. But then where would have been my novel? She did not cry, and Mr Arabin did not melt.' But what is 'the whole truth'? If it is that Mr Arabin is in love with Eleanor, we have already been told that Mr Arabin does not know it himself. If it is the 'whole truth' about what he said to Dr Grantly, can we be sure that we know what it is? Does Trollope imply that Mr Arabin is unconsciously jealous of Mr Slope? When he tells Eleanor that Dr Grantly has the right to advise her about her behaviour, in the same way as Dr Grantly's bishop would have the right to advise the archdeacon about him, is he conferring on Dr Grantly the right of a husband that he secretly wishes to have for himself? The episode remains rather unsatisfactory. Trollope has chosen to place Mr Arabin in an extremely unflattering light.

Mr Arabin, now sure that he loves Eleanor, wants to ask her to marry him, but cannot find words to do so; Eleanor sees that he loves her, but is too angry with him to help him. She 'could not bring herself to abandon her revenge'. This is a deeper and more complex psychological analysis than anything we have been taught to expect by the novel itself. It is, we might think, wonderful improvisation, the complex and subtle creation of conflicting states of feeling, within and between characters who have much in common. How consistent is it with what has gone before? And what effect will these revelations of the pettiness and inadequacy of the author's principally favoured characters have on the mood of this comic novel?

Section Six: The return to Barchester (Chapters 31-4)

The final section of the second volume of the novel concentrates on the plot. The death of the Dean of Barchester opens up a new phase of the war between the church parties at Barchester. The battle for supremacy between the bishop and his wife is dealt with in parenthesis in a night encounter between them which Trollope leaves to the imagination of his readers. The bishop has lost and Mrs Proudie is securely in control. The fête which Miss Thorne is arranging partly in honour of Mr Arabin's arrival is promised for the future and Eleanor's friendly relationship with the Stanhopes is resumed, leaving the way open for Bertie Stanhope to make his advances to her. All of this concentrated action reduces the dialogue sections of the novel and increases the density of the narrative itself.

Against the complexity of the interwoven strands of events, Mr Slope moves forward once again. He dares to believe that he might be Dean of Barchester. It is a fear shared by Archdeacon Grantly and the clergy of the Cathedral. Trollope assembles all these gentlemen and presents them in a passage which suggests the chorus of some Greek play commenting on the likely outcome of a significant event – in this case, the illness of the present Dean. This little passage of dialogue is an excellent example of the dominant comic mode of the novel, which is never wholly submerged by the painful nature of some of the material Trollope introduces into it. The utterance of each of the clergymen is lightly accented like the litanies in their customary service-books. The cathedral clergy and the archdeacon speak to one another antiphonally. And the chancellor supplies a sceptical refrain. Of course, their fears are unfounded and their opinions are wrong. Mr Slope's letters to those he thinks will support him give further evidence of his capacity for being all things to all men: he carefully varies the style of each to suit the expectation of its recipient. But his effrontery in believing himself a suitable candidate for a post which has not yet become vacant shocks the bishop and outrages Mrs Proudie, who has by now taken the measure of Mr Slope. Now Mrs Proudie will do anything to bring about his downfall. Having secured her power over the bishop, she intends to deal with Mr Slope.

But the question of who is to be dean is not likely to be settled in Barchester. Away in Oxford, Dr Gwynne and Tom Staple, Master and Tutor of Lazarus College, respectively, debate the affairs of Barchester as earnestly, and with as little insight, as the clergy of Barchester have done. Equally, they overestimate Mr Slope's power. Pessimistic of the ability of good to triumph by its own power, they mentally shift the pieces on the board, wondering whether Mr Quiverful or Mr Harding should have the Hospital. Tom Staple has a flash of insight: if Mr Quiverful gets the Hospital, why should not Mr Harding be Dean? At the end of Trollope's second volume, part of the possible final picture of the plot is becoming clear.

Section Seven: The Ullathorne Sports (Chapters 35-43)

The third volume of the novel opens with the sports at Ullathorne and offers a mass of new material. Now that one central question has been answered, namely, what will become of Bishop Proudie, we wait for answers to the others. But these – what will become of Eleanor, what will become of Mr Harding, and what will become of Mr Slope – are for the moment lost sight of in a thicket of sub-plots connected with the sports themselves. They have the merit of bringing all the principal characters together; even Dr Gwynne arrives from Oxford. In addition, the tenants and neighbours of the Thornes arrive too, and their steward, Plomacy (who, despite his name, is less than diplomatic), has much to do in keeping out gate-crashers. Trollope finds much comic material in the incongruous social encounters that such an event produces. Who will forget the signora boldly outstaring the Countess De Courcy? (Chapter 37). Some readers, however, will find it difficult to be patient with the social climbing of the Lookalofts, to which Trollope devotes a whole chapter.

The Ullathorne sports are conducted in that comic spirit in which comedy and magic are closely allied. We do not here expect any kind of realism. Ullathorne is as free from the conventions of everyday life as Shakespeare's Forest of Arden. It is here that the question of Eleanor Bold's future is to be settled and the theatrical nature of Trollope's treatment of his material is emphasised by the three chapters entitled 'Ullathorne Sports – Act I, Act II and Act III' which carry the main events of what Trollope calls 'the melodrama which Eleanor was called on to perform this day at Ullathorne'. It has not helped her reputation or her self-esteem that circumstances have forced her to arrive at the party in the same carriage as Mr Slope. She finds herself seated at table between him and Mr Arabin with Bertie Stanhope standing behind her. Despite all the diversions Trollope has introduced into his narrative, our interest is in how he will tell us what is to become of Eleanor. Trollope does not lose the thread of the other main story he has to complete in this volume of the novel. As the bishop says grace over the meal set out for the guests at Ullathorne, the dean of Barchester dies. Trollope tells us that Mr Slope is not in the mind of the Prime Minister who is already thinking about the Dean's successor elsewhere. Once again our expectations are aroused by the machinery of the plot. Who will marry Eleanor, and who will become dean of Barchester?

Before he begins to reveal the answer to the first of these questions, Trollope describes an extraordinary encounter between the signora and Mr Arabin (Chapter 38). It is comparable to the chapter entitled 'A Love Scene' (Chapter 27) in which she pierces the hypocrisy of Mr Slope and exposes the hunger for good things (wealth, rank and the love of beautiful women) which lies beneath his pretended spirituality. With Mr Arabin she is more gentle, but her message is essentially the same. She reads his future as if she were a gipsy in a tent at a fair, contrasting his likely fate with that of the ambitious Mr Slope.

Trollope has endowed the signora with an uncanny insight. We must surely be reminded at this point of the melancholy musings of Mr Arabin at the end of the chapter in which he is introduced to us (Chapter 20). After sparkling 'with his usual unaffected brilliancy' in the archdeacon's drawing room, he 'retired to his bed-room [and] sat there sad, at his open window, repining within himself . . . he was now only vicar of St Ewold's, with a taste for a mitre. Truly he had fallen between two stools.'

The signora does not have much patience with such a weak acquiescence in the life which fate has allotted. While she had harshly delighted in forcing Mr Slope to acknowledge the strength of his own appetites, she does everything she can to turn Mr Arabin away from an unhealthy denial of natural instincts, and urges him 'to take a man's wages also'. In the context of the scene, it is surely right to infer that the wages the signora has in mind refer to the due rewards of love as well as to those of professional endeavour. Here in the mouth of the signora, Trollope has put words which perhaps come near to his own views of what is worth pursuing in life.

And yet in Mr Arabin, Signora Neroni has met her match. She flirts with him and indulges in the facile chatter which is her stock-in-trade. And yet she cannot alter his nature which, however, susceptible to her feminine charm, cannot be diverted from an attachment to the truth. He tells her candidly that he is in love with Eleanor Bold, and Trollope's narrator records her reflections thus: 'She felt that she never could induce Mr Arabin to make protestations to her that were not true, or to listen to nonsense that was mere nonsense.' This tribute to truth in the mouth of the disreputable, the worldly woman's acknowledgement of the force of the ideal which Mr Arabin embodies, is not easy to set aside. Looked at through Signora Neroni's cynical eyes, the preoccupations of Barchester seem deluded and absurd. Yet even she has to admit that the politics of the church are incidental to its central values which are completely opposed to the pursuit of power in which so many of the Barchester clergy are engaged.

Trollope does not linger over these more solemn implications of his novel. The second act of Eleanor's melodrama consists in Mr Slope's ludicrous proposal to her which culminates in her slapping his face. Trollope is not content to humiliate him as a lover: the real aims of his religious professions are unmasked in the process:

> He longed in his heart to be preaching at her. 'Twas thus that he was ordinarily avenged of sinning mortal men and women. Could he at once have ascended his Sunday rostrum and fulminated at her such denunciations as his spirit delighted in, his bosom would have been greatly eased.

Truly, there is something Satanic about Mr Slope.

Having described this episode in detail, Trollope swings the machinery of his plot back into bustling activity. Mr Slope departs to Barchester on learning of the death of the dean, not omitting to make himself known to Dr Gwynne before he goes. Mr Harding goes back to Plumstead, promising to explain to the Grantlys how Eleanor really feels about Mr Slope. The party breaks up. Bertie saves Eleanor from the embarrassment of returning in Mr Slope's carriage so that he can take the opportunity which his sister has pressed upon him, to propose to Eleanor himself. This busyness is characteristic of the bursts of farcical activity which Trollope likes to arrange for his people. Even as Eleanor goes with Charlotte Stanhope in search of Bertie, Trollope feels compelled to describe in detail how Mr Arabin is once more caught in the toils of the signora's charms and how Eleanor sees him hovering helplessly over the signora's sofa – the champion of truth apparently floundering in temptation, and no help to the romantic heroine, who is being led off to face her second ordeal. But Bertie's proposal has no heart in it: it is insulting because of its indifference. He is as relieved as she is that nothing will come of it. And so she reaches Barchester safely, still free to accept the right man, if he has the courage to present himself.

Section Eight: Concluding (Chapters 43-53)

The twisting course of Trollope's plot is not quite finished yet: first, the Quiverfuls are satisfied and Dr Gwynne sees for himself that Mrs Proudie is all-powerful at the Palace. Mr Slope's hopes of the deanery are temporarily inflated by an article in *The Jupiter*, giving him the newspaper's support. Trollope devotes a chapter ('Mrs Bold at Home') to a description of Eleanor's sadness and her father's philosophical acceptance of his apparently reduced circumstances. Half of the following chapter is devoted to the despatch of Bertie Stanhope to Italy and in what remains of it the signora tells Eleanor that Mr Arabin loves her. Not all of Trollope's complex narrative can be brought to a smooth conclusion; nor does its liveliness necessarily compensate for its untidiness. The signora's humiliation of Mr Slope in the presence of Mr Thorne and Mr Arabin is rendered with a savagery which does full justice to her malicious sarcasm, but the ludicrous botch of Mr Thorne's meeting with the signora's daughter ('the last of the Neros') undermines any claim to seriousness that the signora might make for herself. Mr Arabin's conduct with the signora has raised a question about his probity in the minds of the Grantlys. But the official offer of the deanery to Mr Harding settles the fate of Mr Slope. Trollope, however, is never short of questions to be raised. Will Mr Harding accept the position he has been offered?

For two chapters (Chapters 48-9) Trollope moves back in time. We learn that on the very day that Mr Thorne was witnessing the humiliation of Mr Slope, Miss Thorne was inviting Eleanor to Ullathorne with the intention of bringing her and Mr Arabin together. Not content with weaving the threads of his stories into one complex pattern, Trollope has no hesitation about tacking on to his material a completely new strip, if it seems necessary to complete his story. The signora has been used to make each of the lovers aware of their love for one another: now Miss Thorpe brings them physically together. Even in his treatment of the sequence of events that brings the lovers together, Trollope displays his capacity for expanding his material. We learn in the fifth paragraph of Chapter 48 that Mr Arabin has proposed: but Trollope does not believe his readers will be satisfied without a detailed dramatic rendering of the proposal and its subsequent scenes of tenderness, which include, of course, the announcement of the engagement to Eleanor's surprised and delighted father. Trollope enjoys a surprise and endlessly exploits it: Mr Harding surprises Dr Grantly with the news; Dr Grantly surprises Mr Arabin with his knowledge of it. Mrs Quiverful is surprised by Dr Grantly's unexpected kindness to her. The luxuriant tendrils of Trollope's narrative spread everywhere. Indeed, he complains himself of the difficulty of bringing matters to a satisfactory conclusion ('Who can apportion out and dovetail his incidents, dialogues, characters, and descriptive morsels, so as to fit them all exactly into 930 pages [the number of pages in the first edition], without either compressing them unnaturally, or extending them artificially at the end of his labour?' – Chapter 51).

Trollope cannot end his novel without a final encounter between Mr Slope and Mrs Proudie, whose verbal triumphing over him ('Fie, Mr. Slope, Fie! You an evangelical clergyman indeed!') must be as bitter to him as her insulting offer to make him Mr Quiverful's curate at Puddingdale. Dr Gwynne is once more appealed to as a powerful intermediary with government to translate into reality Mr Harding's ambition to make Mr Arabin dean of Barchester. And Mr Harding is given a prolonged little scene in which he can surprise Mr Arabin with the news. So that no tincture of ill-will should be left in the lees of this long novel, Trollope has Mr Harding personally introduce Mr Quiverful as the new Warden of Hiram's Hospital. As Trollope tells us, 'the end of a novel, like the end of a children's dinner-party, must be made up of sweetmeats and sugar-plums'. He tells us of the Arabins' wedding, of the Archdeacon's generosity, of the agreement of the Proudies to attend to the affairs of the diocese and leave the cathedral clergymen alone. Mrs Arabin and Mrs Grantly have found a new pleasure in their sisterly relationship. The Stanhopes go back to Italy. Mr Harding is left in the serenity of virtuous old age. We have already been told in detail of Mr Slope's future fate in London. The threads of the novel, lovingly drawn out, have finally been tied together.

Part 4

Hints for study

THE FIRST ESSENTIAL HINT for the study of literary texts is that the student should read and re-read the work in question. He (or she) should read it critically, approaching it with questions which have been raised by those successive readings. The aim of this book is to provoke and stimulate such questions in the mind of the reader and to distinguish, where this is possible, questions that can be definitely answered from those where the evidence and grounds for judgement are not clear. Many of the factual questions will have been answered by the glossaries which accompany the summaries of each chapter of the novel. Some questions of a more general type will have been answered in the introduction. On a first reading, we naturally want to know what happens, we want to laugh at the jokes, to sympathise with some characters, to laugh at others and to detest one or two. The reader's curiosity can be satisfied, and his sympathies aroused, without every word of the text having been read.

Later readings are likely to be more reflective. We might wonder how historically accurate the novel is. Has it been conducted according to a precise time-table, or are its frequently mentioned months and dates only roughly accurate? What sort of institution was the Church of England at the time Trollope was writing? How significant a part of the life of the English man or woman of the time was it? How significant was it to Trollope himself?

Not all of these questions are strictly literary, nor can they all be answered simply by reading the novel itself. Some would take us to histories of the time, or to the letters and biographies of which Victorians were so fond. But there are other, more strictly literary questions. What kind of novel is *Barchester Towers*? What interests or appetites does it arouse in the reader, and how does it satisfy them? What sympathies does it seek to engage: does it appear to invite the reader to make judgements? What judgements does it expect him to accept, or to acquiesce in? Answers to questions of this kind are likely to be made against our knowledge of other novels, or of other literature in general. We compare our reading of Trollope's novel with the mental picture we have of the novel as such. Or, less consciously, we read it with a set of expectations developed in us by the reading of other novels. *Barchester Towers* was originally published in three volumes and much attention has been paid in the previous part of these

Notes to the way in which the material of the novel has been shaped to fit this pattern. As we know, *Barchester Towers* is the sequel to *The Warden* (1855) and, although it can be understood without any knowledge of the earlier work, some of the features of *The Warden* are carried over to the second novel. Each of these novels is very consciously literary. Reference is made to Shakespeare and to other poets; there are elements of parody; there are, in particular, many references to the famous epics of Greek and Latin literature. The prose in which these novels are written is not elaborate, but it is cadenced and conscious of itself, too unobtrusively witty ever to be called 'plain'. Consider the passage from the first chapter in which the last days of the dying bishop and of the Tory government are described ('At this time the bishop was quite on his last legs; but the ministry also were tottering . . . '). The description is mannered and witty, though it may not be too easy to put one's finger on what makes it so. Essentially, it is constructed on the amusing parallelism between the life of the bishop and life of the government. Neither is expected to last long, but each lasts longer than expected. Dr Grantly has returned from Oxford with the hint from Dr Gwynne that he will succeed his father – but only if the appointment is made by a Tory government. If they are ousted by the Whigs, the new prime minister will appoint their own man. The death of the bishop and the fall of the government may not keep in step with one another. Trollope is exact about the measurement of time – the bishop is given a month, then another fortnight, then no more than a week. But by that time the government has only five days. It looks as if the bishop will win the race by staying alive, and the archdeacon will lose the bishopric. The parallelism of the two events is also mirrored in the syntax: 'bishop' mirrors 'ministry' and 'on his last legs' chimes with 'tottering'. Notice, too, the rhythm of 'to resume his place in the palace' and 'to continue to perform for the father' and 'the last duties of a son'. Notice the alliteration of 'place' and 'palace' and 'perform' and the balancing of 'father' and 'son'. Look at the slight play of words on 'lived on wine alone' and 'still lived', the first meaning 'feed, supply oneself with food', the second meaning 'to be capable of vital function'. Notice again the alliteration on 'sustaining modicum of madeira': Trollope just lightly emphasises how little wine was needed to keep the bishop alive and how ironic it was that the son, faithfully helping to keep his father alive, was worldly enough to wonder whether he might die in time to allow his son to succeed him. Too much of this kind of verbal self-consciousness would weary the reader, and Trollope breaks away from it, employing a style which is rapid, conversational, and off-hand.

These subtle, detailed verbal nuances help to create the *tone* of Trollope's prose. But it must not be forgotten that there are many tones – Trollope's prose is flexible and capable of many effects. Here tone means 'tone of voice' and it is the tone of the narrator's voice, or perhaps we should say the tone of the narrative, which is sometimes distinctly and deliberately personal, directly addressing the reader and sometimes impersonal, withdrawn to a simple record of imagined events. But if the reader looks closely at how this story is told, he will become very aware of the personality, and the prejudices, of this very opinionated narrator. The effect of 'tone' is that our perception of what is described or imagined is limited and guided by a deliberate artistic choice of the author. He has chosen to write this passage in a way that makes the bishop's death appear slightly comical. The outlandish names of the doctors (a random selection of names of consecutive letters of the Greek alphabet) reinforce this sense of comedy – they are highly impressive nonentities. Seen through this artful prose, Dr Grantly at his father's death-bed is a comic figure. Our attention is diverted from the conventional responses we might make to this situation by the small stylistic effects which signal the necessary distancing of comedy.

But, of course, Trollope is far from being simply comedic. Certainly, there is a comic side to the frustrating situation in which Dr Grantly finds himself. There is also a more poignant aspect. There is another view of him taken as he sits by his father's bed, asking himself whether he is longing for his father's death. This passage is quite different in tone. We notice the not quite usual inversion of the first sentence – 'by no means easy were the emotions of him who sat watching'. The inversion itself is a balanced response to the final sentence of the previous paragraph which refers to the easiness of the bishop's passage from life to death. But Trollope perhaps wants to re-focus our attention on Dr Grantly and thus does not simply refer to him by name but specifically refers to his 'watching' (and, we may think, his waiting). The 'it' in the next sentence refers to his own promotion. Notice how easily the sentences that follow seem to mimic the archdeacon's thinking, though there is nothing specifically which would cause us to infer this unless it is that correction from 'who was now in' to 'who was soon to be out'. The anxious apprehensiveness of the archdeacon's thinking seems to be caught by the change. It is enough to make him realise that he is only thinking of himself. The next snapshot of the archdeacon shows the effort he is making to humble his pride.

So we are not dealing simply with a puppet, or a figure of fun, seen from the outside. Trollope's tone here conveys the empathy he has (and means to arouse in us) for this opinionated, aggressive, sometimes rather stupid man who has nevertheless a warm spot of feeling in his heart, strong loyalty to his order and to his class, and sound judgement about clerical matters. Trollope can make fun of him because of his considerable limitations: do we approve of him because he has the support of the author? Perhaps that is not a proper question to ask, because it would take us beyond the area of literature into politics. At least we can notice that Trollope makes no attempt to weigh the faults and virtues of the characters in a common scale, as Jane Austen does. Archdeacon Grantly's social position may not protect him from all criticism, but Trollope is not eager to make any connection between private virtue and the health of society.

It is not surprising that a consideration of the tone of the novel should have led us into a discussion of some of its themes. If *tone* is the means by which the novelist guides our perceptions, *theme* is what, more broadly considered, he wants us to see. Are there any themes in *Barchester Towers*, or are there only events? The critical commentary has stressed Trollope's fascination with 'plot', with the complex interconnectedness of human affairs, the astonishing way in which chance rules human life so that hopes are defeated, expectations dashed, assumptions shown to be unfounded. But life is not just a game of snakes-and-ladders. Some outcomes are more favourable than others: there are some whom we want to see winning, others we hope will lose. It is the business of the novelist, Trollope's practice seems to imply, to satisfy these desires. What system of values is revealed when this process is applied by the novelist to the operation of chance in human affairs?

Trollope makes no analysis of his own system of values: he simply displays it in action. From the action of the novel, then, some conclusion may be drawn about his themes. Perhaps they can best be described by saying that Trollope holds a two-world theory of how human life operates. The first world is that of unchecked desire and appetite. This world operates partly by the law of chance, partly by the principle that victory goes to the strong. The novel, as we have seen, opens in a world where these conditions operate, but Archdeacon Grantly immediately recognises that other laws (the love a son should have for his father, for example) have a greater claim on him. Perhaps it is worth noticing that Trollope seems equally interested in the different psychological effect that choosing to live in one or other of these worlds has on human beings. The archdeacon's wish to be a bishop may lead him to wish for the death of his father. He recognises that such a wish is wrong, and asks forgiveness, but he is not thereby led into the second world that Trollope seems to imagine. This is a world of unselfish goodness and humility. Perhaps only one of his characters, Mr Harding, can be said to live fully in this world. It is a world in which human beings are motivated by an active will to seek what is good. Such an active goodwill is not necessarily equipped with the power to see what is good. Human beings are limited creatures: even Mr Harding's insight into the feelings and motives of his daughter is limited. Because he has not a clear grasp of her nature, he is not able to prevent some of the distress and unpleasantness we have already noticed in the middle section of the novel where Eleanor Bold's feelings for Mr Slope are misunderstood by her family. But in the end the steady radiance of Mr Harding's good-will prevails against his intellectual shortcomings and his failures of sensitivity. Perhaps it will be worth considering each of the main characters in relationship to these two worlds – let us call them the world of will and the world of grace. And let us be prepared to consider that there might be a third, which we can call the world of art. Rapidly surveying the list of Trollope's characters (from the De Courcys to the Lookalofts), it does not seem impossible to fit them all into one or the other category, except for one group. The Stanhopes, or at least some of them, strive neither for worldly goods nor for the good that is beyond this world. Their values are purely aesthetic: they live not to use or to be used, to win or lose, but to be admired. So let us say they (or some of them) live in a world of art.

Mr Harding

The word 'grace' has many theological connotations. All that is meant by it here may be found in the definition of it given in the *Oxford English Dictionary* which is 'the divine influence which operates in men to regenerate and sanctify, to inspire virtuous impulses, and to impart strength to endure trial and to resist temptation'. Of course, Mr Hardy is a clergyman; he has been ordained and initiated into all the means of grace which the worship and sacraments of the church could bestow on him. In particular he is devoted to the music of the church, which Mr Slope in his cathedral sermon called 'the meretricious charm of melody'.

In the second chapter of *Barchester Towers* Mr Harding is reintroduced to Trollope's reader as a sensitive man who had made a 'disinterested sacrifice' of his wardenship for the benefit of the old men who were the beneficiaries of Hiram's will. He had not asked for anything in return, even when the Archbishop of Canterbury had hinted that some or other benefice might be available to him. He continued to visit the old men he had once looked after, and lived above a shop in the High Street of Barchester, peaceable, charitable, and humble. He is not so humble, however, as to be prepared to ask Mr Slope to help him to regain the Hospital. Trollope does not attempt to convince us that Mr Harding is a saint: he is capable of anger. But he does not attempt to convert his angry feelings into hostile action.

When the archdeacon wonders what they are to do with Mr Slope and how they are to get rid of him, Mr Harding says, 'I don't suppose he can do us much harm.' His poor opinion of Mr Slope is based on a strong disapproval of his lack of courtesy. As he says, 'Christian ministers are never called on by God's word to insult the convictions, or even the prejudices of their brethren.'

A crucial scene for the character of Mr Harding is his interview with Mr Slope about the Hospital. Mr Slope has made no secret of his belief that everything Mr Harding represents is out of date. Mr Harding, old, unassertive, conscious of the certainty of death, turns to his religion for support. There is nothing dogmatic, or other-worldly, about Mr Harding's notion of religion: it is based on the goodness of natural things and finds its fulfilment in harmonious personal relationships. But to prevent any suggestion of mawkishness in his character, Trollope's next sentence reads, 'Nevertheless, he did not like to be thus kept waiting', and it is because he finally rouses Mr Harding to anger that Mr Slope is able to find an excuse to represent to the bishop that he has refused the wardenship. Notice however how courteously the anger is expressed: 'I shall consult my friends . . . I shall decline the situation if I find that any such conditions are attached to it as those you have suggested.'

The elaborate syntax of the sentence combines plainness of speech with the intricate web of implication that is woven by a succession of dependent clauses. It is too much for Mr Slope who simplifies its provisional statement into an outright rejection of the wardenship.

Trollope's analysis of Mr Harding's character is acute. He is a man who has outlived his time. He has no taste for an England where men can be unscrupulous and conduct is judged by a crude yardstick of worldly success. At the same time he is vulnerable enough to doubt his own worth, and to question his own standards. He is willing to repent of his own shortcomings but does he have the moral strength to endure the suffering which such repentance might entail? Trollope makes much of Mr Harding's weakness of character, his conscientiousness, his meekness, his self-doubt. But, again and again, these weaknesses are shown to be the basis of his virtues. His toleration of the idea of a possible marriage between Eleanor and Mr Slope springs from the fact that 'in his charity he did not hate the chaplain as the archdeacon did, and as we do'. As Trollope makes clear in Chapter 28 Mr Harding loves his daughter too much to blame her even if she wants to marry Mr Slope.

So, in Mr Harding's weakness, there is wisdom. He does not want to ask Eleanor outright what her feelings are. If she were to admit that she loved Mr Slope, a marriage between them would be made more likely. To remain silent might be the wisest way of preventing it from happening. In Chapter 36 Trollope makes a point of clearing up the matter between Eleanor and her father, but Mr Harding takes little further part in the novel until he is offered the deanery. Once more, Trollope returns to the theme of Mr Harding's sense of his own unfitness. As Trollope's narrator puts it (in Chapter 47):

> Mr Harding seemed to have a foolish idea, not only that there were new duties to do, but that no one should accept the place who was not himself prepared to do them.

He is content to find such a man in Mr Arabin. The last word on Mr Harding's character may be left to one of the old men whom, as warden of the hospital, he had so tenderly looked after. In response to Mr Quiverful's admission that he could 'never be the same well-loved friend and father that [Mr Harding] has been', old Bunce says:

> 'No, sir, no' . . . 'no one can be that. Not if the new bishop sent a hangel to us out of heaven. We doesn't doubt you'll do your best, sir, but you'll not be like the old master; not to us old ones.'

The Grantlys

As archdeacon, Dr Grantly is one of the managers of the church. During the time when his father was bishop, he ran the affairs of the diocese. In that respect he acted on behalf of the bishop just in the way Mr Slope hopes to act for Bishop Proudie. Dr Grantly, however, is a gentleman. He belongs by birth and education to a class of people who see themselves as natural rulers. He has the highest respect for the power of the Church and 'regards things temporal as being by their nature subject to those which are spiritual'. But he does not despise the good things of life. He is tolerant and broad-minded about conduct so long as there is no doubt about belief or about loyalty to the Church. He is undoubtedly authoritarian, dogmatic and a little insensitive. But although Trollope sees the flaws in his character, he regards the archdeacon as an essentially sound, if limited, member of his class. Mr Harding's sweetness of character must be supplemented by some more vigorous and forthright quality, if the Church is to resist Evangelical influences which might undermine it from within. Dr Grantly is hasty in temper and sometimes irascible in speech, as when he is expressing his opinion of Mr Slope in Chapter 6.

He is vigorous, unrestrained, sure of his own opinion, ready to jump to conclusions. His instinctive reaction to Bishop Proudie and Mr Slope is to oppose them even if this means going to unreasonable extremes in adopting theological opinions and practices which they would abhor. He is responsible for recruiting Mr Arabin for his battle against Mr Slope, but he sees him merely as an instrument of war. How easily his passions can be turned against his friends can be seen in his treatment of Eleanor Bold. When she attempts to put in a good word for Mr Slope, the archdeacon 'turn[s] on her with almost brutal wrath'. His suspicions about Eleanor's feelings for Mr Slope produce some of the most painful scenes in the novel. Archdeacon Grantly is fiercely partisan: unlike his father-in-law, he can only love where he approves. Of course, there is much social snobbery in his attitudes. He believes in that close solidarity of a class or order which regards those who do not belong to it as hopeless outsiders.

Despite the imperfections of his character, it must be remembered that Archdeacon Grantly is a comic character. The fact that he takes himself so seriously merely adds to the comic effect. When he learns of Eleanor's intention to marry Mr Arabin, he feels annoyance that he never expected such a marriage, surprise that he should have been so blind and a growing satisfaction that all should have turned out well. Trollope treats each of these emotions at some length, drawing out for our amusement the succession of discordant feelings that pass through the archdeacon's breast. But his triumph over Mr Slope fills him with 'supreme good humour' and 'he made a great resolve that he would atone to Eleanor for all the injury he had done her by the munificence of her future treatment'.

Mrs Grantly, the archdeacon's wife and the sister of Eleanor Bold, shares her husband's prejudices. She cannot be said to be any more perceptive than he is, but she is much less aggressive. It is she who first suggests a possible marriage between her sister and Mr Slope. She is every inch a suitable wife for a worldly clergyman: she is sharp, clear-headed and full of practical sense. As Trollope says, 'No one knew better than Mrs Grantly the appurtenances necessary to a comfortable house'. But she is always ready to acknowledge the supremacy of her husband.

The Proudies

Bishop and Mrs Proudie are that inseparable couple, the hen-pecked husband and the masterful wife. Although they are both said to be connected with the aristocracy, the reader is more likely to remember his weakness and her vulgarity. Trollope provides a plausible picture of Bishop Proudie. He is one of the new men, used to moving in official circles, close to royal favour, not an old-fashioned Tory but broad-minded, tolerant, active in many committees. Trollope's presentation of the bishop's past history is somewhat at variance with his picture of the bishop in Barchester. The virtues which have enabled him to rise to his present position are little in evidence during the action of the novel.

On his first appearance he is completely dominated by Mrs Proudie and Mr Slope who scarcely allow him to address a word to the archdeacon. We see him through the archdeacon's eyes for whom he is 'so contemptible a creature . . . that he could not condescend to discuss his character. He was a puppet to be played by others; a mere wax doll, done up in an apron and a shovel hat, to be stuck on a throne or elsewhere, and pulled about by wires as others chose'. From one narrow point of view *Barchester Towers* tells the story of the Bishop's attempt to achieve independence. His chances of success never look good: under strain, he suffers from bilious attacks and prefers to delegate difficult tasks to his subordinates. When his wife and Mr Slope are in combat, he is content to remain silent. Bishop Proudie rarely rises above the level of low comedy. He is abject, spineless, cowardly, ill at ease.

Mrs Proudie is opposed to her husband in every way. Trollope makes it clear from the beginning that there is little happiness in the bishop's household because of Mrs Proudie's authoritarian disposition. As he puts it, 'in matters domestic she rules over her titular lord, and rules with a rod of iron . . . But Mrs Proudie is not satisfied with such home dominion, and stretches her power over all [the bishop's] movements, and will not even abstain from things spiritual'. Mrs Proudie is not a complex character, and Trollope agrees that he has not portrayed her as 'an agreeable or an amiable lady'. Only in her dealings with Mr Quiverful does she appear to have qualities that we can admire. For the most part Trollope uses her as the 'female devil' in his novel – the dark, unlikeable character whom his readers are expected to detest. Perhaps she can be seen as an early example of a feminist – a woman of considerable force of character and ability, who is unable to hold a place in the world because the world refuses to take such women seriously. Since she is by nature opposed to the established system, Trollope chooses to make her a figure of fun. She is a woman who wants to possess some of the privileges normally reserved for men. She is freakish, perhaps even dangerous. Thus she must be made to look foolish. As a supporter of Evangelical opinion, she is a danger to the traditions of Barchester. She prefers Mr Slope's sermons to the way Mr Harding sings the litany which she describes as 'play-acting'.

Trollope makes it impossible for the reader to take Mrs Proudie seriously by arranging for her farcical public humiliation at her own reception at the hands of Bertie Stanhope. Attempting to increase the flow of traffic round the signora's sofa, he gives it a push into the middle of the room, where it tears away a large part of the lace train of Mrs Proudie's dress. Trollope describes the incident in exaggerated language, comparing the destruction of the dress to the collapse of some fortification. In the war between Barchester and the Proudies it is a moment of symbolic significance. Before the evening is over she has been insulted by the signora who laughs at her claim to be 'always equally averse to impropriety of conduct of every description'. For the rest of the novel Mrs Proudie's sphere of influence is restricted to the domestic field. Her battle is not with Barchester but with the bishop and Mr Slope. She defeats both, but her victory is at her own expense. Mr Slope has been her creation and is meant to be her instrument. She is outraged to find that he has a mind and a will of his own. She is particularly outraged at his interest in the signora. Mr Slope betrays her, but in doing so, he reveals the narrowly puritanical idealism which is the basis of her view of what human conduct should be.

Mr Slope

It is impossible to disentangle the interlocking characters of the bishop, Mrs Proudie and Mr Slope. Together they form the central mechanism of the novel. If Mrs Proudie is 'the female devil', Mr Slope is her male counterpart. He is, however, a more sinister figure than Mrs Proudie: we are obliged to take him more seriously. Where she blusters and storms, he works slyly and insidiously, menacing the security of 'the female angel', Eleanor Bold. There is something satanic about Mr Slope, which goes beyond the merely personally disagreeable. Trollope gives him red hair and clammy hands. His face is red and his nose looks 'as though it had been cleverly formed out of a red-coloured cork'. He is inordinately vain; he is preoccupied with fantasies about his own future. His principal interest is the pursuit of power. He habitually prevaricates as we can see when he misrepresents Mr Harding to the bishop and when he tries to retract his offer of the wardenship to Mr Quiverful. Perhaps the least agreeable of his characteristics is his capacity for hate. Trollope links it to his Evangelicalism in a specially damning way, as in the scene with Eleanor when she slaps his cheek in refusing his offer of marriage.

Trollope makes us aware of the underside of Mr Slope's vehement morality. Preaching is the vehicle of his vengeance. His momentary insight into his own faults brings him no sense of humility. He must rise above the world of ordinary mortals and, from a position of moral superiority, shower them with his indignation. A similar psychological effect is produced when he is publicly humiliated by the signora (Chapter 46). Hatred rather than love is the special note of the Evangelicals in *Barchester Towers*: the contrast with Mr Harding cannot be missed. We may compare these descriptions of the rage of Mr Slope with how Mrs Proudie thinks of a possible improvement in the morals of the signora: 'Mrs Proudie looked on the Signora as one of the lost . . . and was therefore able to enjoy the luxury of hating her, without the drawback of wishing her eventually well out of her sins.'

The Quiverfuls

The Quiverfuls are the objects of action in the novel rather than agents, though Mrs Quiverful has the energy of spirit which comes from a lifetime's effort to bring up her large family decently on the small stipend that her husband enjoys. There is something heroic about her journey to Barchester on a farmer's cart to see the bishop's wife. She has no shame about the vigour with which she presses her case. She had but one feeling, and that was confined to her family. She cares little how she twists and turns among these newcomers at the bishop's palace so long as she can twist her husband into the warden's house.

Poverty, on the other hand, has depressed Mr Quiverful. He feels sad at the thought of supplanting Mr Harding as warden of the Hospital, but he has no spirit to be other than 'civil, cringingly civil' to Mr Slope. A clergyman with four hundred pounds per annum and fourteen children to bring up has no alternative but to consider his material interests.

The Stanhopes

Of all the characters in *Barchester Towers* the Stanhope family are the most dangerous to the ethos of Barchester. Dr Stanhope is a conventional enough absentee clergyman, brought home by moral persuasion rather than by any legal sanction, since the Acts of Parliament which forbade non-resident clergy did not apply to those who enjoyed these privileges at the time. The Stanhopes' principal family characteristic was heartlessness but, as Trollope says, '[it] was, in most of them, accompanied by so great an amount of good nature as to make itself but little noticeable to the world'. Mrs Stanhope regards 'a state of inactivity as the only earthly good' and lives mainly to be well dressed. Charlotte Stanhope is mistress of the household and regards her father's livings simply as a source of income. She has no religious feeling whatsoever.

The principal members of the family for the purpose of the novel are Bertie Stanhope, the feckless and idle son of the family, and Madeline, the Signora Neroni. Bertie is talented but fickle, open to every influence, unable to persist for long in any settled course of action. He suffers from a complete inability to recognise the hierarchy of rank and station. Despite stating all his defects plainly, Trollope finds much comedy in the effect Bertie has on Barchester society, above all in his wonderfully impertinent conversation with Dr Proudie at Mrs Proudie's reception.

It is unlikely that Bertie will stick long to anything and his religious preferences are based, we might suspect, on an aesthetic principle. Bertie Stanhope has no character: he is simply a series of attitudes without any binding purpose. He is perfectly prepared to contemplate marrying Eleanor Bold for her money, but when the time comes for him to make his proposal (in Chapter 42) he clumsily tells her he is acting in the interests of his family. He is only asking her to marry him because his sister has suggested the idea.

The signora is a far more significant character in the novel. In her person the heartless nihilism of the Stanhope family is concentrated. From her sofa she observes the world as a bizarre comedy. She has reduced what human beings might value to three essentials – money, sex and power. She takes nothing else seriously: all idealism is a pathetic mask for the face of human greed. Men and woman only count with her to the extent that they are willing to acknowledge their fundamental adherence to material interests. Trollope wonderfully describes this shattered beauty so that she has some of the characteristics of a fabled enchantress – woman from the waist up, something unpleasant, almost sinister from waist to foot. His exaggerated description of the signora is perfectly suited to the melodramatic language she herself employs. It is quite consistent with the signora's own fantasies about her rank, her name and her daughter's relationship to an 'old Roman family from which the worst of the Caesar's sprang.' At Mrs Proudie's reception, the signora in her white velvet dress, with a band of red velvet with a Cupid in mosaic at the centre of it, is the object of everyone's attention. Dr Proudie, Mr Slope, Mr Arabin, even Mr Thorne are all subject to her fascination: her sofa is a kind of spider's web to which men are irresistibly attracted. To Mrs Proudie she is 'an intriguing Italian woman, half wife and half not, full of affectation, airs and impudence', 'a painted Jezebel'. It is Mr Slope's interest in the signora, too publicly demonstrated at the reception, that opens up the first crack in the alliance between him and Mrs Proudie.

Trollope's treatment of the flirtation between Mr Slope and the signora is beautifully managed. On the one hand he makes it clear how wholly unfit the signora is as an object of serious male attention: her husband is alive, she has no money, her lameness makes her unsuitable 'as the wife of any man who wanted a useful mate'. But Mr Slope is passionate; and she loves to exercise her power over men. Trollope's metaphors underline her cruelty: she is a spider who catches flies, although she has no use for her victims when caught. She pins Mr

Slope down as boys pin insects on a cork, 'that she might enjoy the energetic agony of his gyrations'.

In Chapter 27 ('A Love Scene') Trollope gives us the first of the brilliantly created encounters between Mr Slope and the signora. As he stumbles through his repertoire of accepted banalities which are supposed to pass between a lover and his mistress, she forces him to face the realities of their situation. What disgusts her is the romantic idealisation of a love which she sees as squalid and he regards as desirable but unattainable.

Despite the comic setting, there is, as the narrator allows, a serious dimension to this exchange. Whatever the signora's experiences in marriage may have been, she speaks of the reality of sexual commitment in a challenging and startlingly modern way. She is more radical than Mr Slope: she does not reject his romanticism, but she presses his language to its limit, demanding that his words should be justified by his actions. Of course, she knows that they will not be so justified, and her own language is permeated with bitterness, cynicism and despair. The alternative to an impossible love is the enjoyment of what the world has to offer. Of course, she already suspects that for Mr Slope the possible goods of this world include Eleanor Bold. It is not until Chapter 46 that the signora's tormenting of Mr Slope is done in public before two other men, Mr Arabin and Mr Thorne, who have risen to the bait of her attractions. Notice how beautifully Trollope arranges that the episode should arise out of the hostility that has come about between Mr Thorne and Mr Slope as a result of the fascination which the signora exercises on them both. Trollope first allows Mr Slope to have a joke at the expense of the older, worthier, more influential man. Then there is another laugh against Mr Thorne when he unsuccessfully tries to be nice to the signora's little girl. Mr Slope has smiled once too often: the signora takes her revenge. First she teases him with his hopes of the deanery, then she taunts him with his proposal to Eleanor Bold. She concludes with her mocking song:

> It's gude to be off with the old love – Mr Slope,
> Before you are on with the new –

making it bitterly clear to all how far he had gone in professing an attachment to herself.

In the light of her own disappointed hopes of love, it is more understandable, though not less to the signora's credit, that she has the honesty – and the disinterestedness – to recognise the true affection that Mr Arabin and Eleanor have for one another. In their relationship she sees an image of the enduring love which is the converse of her bitter cynicism. Here is the 'singular question' she puts to Eleanor in Chapter 45: 'Do you love him, love him with all your heart and soul, with all the love your bosom can feel? For I can tell you that he loves you . . . What would I not give to be loved in such a way by such a man, that is, if I were an object fit for any man to love!'

There is a pathos in that last remark that is difficult to ignore. Part of this extreme loathing the signora feels is for herself. It is projected as hate on people she despises. It stems from an ideal of human perfection which, since it cannot be attained, is converted into hate. The signora threatens everything Barchester stands for, but even she acknowledges the good when she sees it.

The landed interest: the Thornes, De Courcys, Lookalofts and Greenacres

Miss Thorne's *fête champêtre* brings into the novel a new set of characters whose relevance to its main themes may appear rather difficult to determine. The Thornes have already been introduced in Chapter 22. Trollope introduces them with an ironic mockery which is not finally sustained throughout the chapter. They are eccentrics: they are ridiculously old-fashioned, but in the end, they are the salt of the earth. What they represent are traditional upper-class English virtues, which flow from the continuous possession of land for many hundreds of years. The Thornes love to trace their ancestry to before the Norman Conquest. They are ancestor worshippers; they love the sense of continuity and the civilised decorum which space, wealth and order have produced. Their culture has been enhanced by the development of literature in the eighteenth century. They both relish the socially restricted ordered elegance which was characteristic of that time. They have resisted change. To that extent they are allies of Mr Harding against the innovations of Mr Slope. But these matters hardly touch them. For them church-going is a further aspect of their settled way of life: its religious significance has been assimilated in their worship of the past.

In the light of the Thornes' family tradition, the De Courcys (whose name reveals their link with the Normans) are newcomers. They are rude, condescending, inconsiderate. They are of higher rank than the Thornes, but that is nothing to those who prize length of lineage above wealth or social position. Mrs Proudie and the Countess De Courcy are glad to exchange disparaging remarks about their hosts. Once again, the signora refuses to be impressed: she is perfectly capable of outstaring the Countess.

The Lookalofts and the Greenacres enact in miniature the struggle between the old and the new which is the central theme of the novel. Mrs Greenacre's perception of the presumption of Mrs Lookaloft, who has decided to consort with the gentry in Miss Thorne's drawing-room, instead of keeping to the paddock which has been allotted to people of her class, is succinctly expressed, but her indignation is answered phlegmatically by her husband: 'Now I like this place better, cause I be more at home like, and don't have to pay for them fine clothes for the missus. Everyone to his taste . . . and if neighbour Lookaloft thinks that he has the best of it, he's welcome.'

The squabble for social distinction at this level is a matter for broad comedy. Too great an insistence on social decorum leads to injustice and bad feeling in the end, as Mr Thorne's ill-named steward, Plomacy, finds as he tries to keep gate-crashers out of the party. Miss Thorne, after all, has instructed him not to be too particular about admitting the people of the area. The Ullathorne sports are meant to be a joyful gathering of all classes brought together in the fabled social harmony of Merrie England. Not everything goes right there; but the disharmonies and infelicities of the day – from Bob Greenacre's tumble at the quintain to Eleanor's unwanted proposals of marriage – are simply a prelude to the harmonies to come. The false synthesis of a revived medievalism gives way to a true expression of contemporary value, symbolised by the marriage of Mr Arabin and Eleanor and the restoration of ecclesiastical order in Barchester.

Some specimen questions

(1) Much of the comedy in *Barchester Towers* depends on Trollope's skilful employment of different styles of language. Discuss.

(2) Is *Barchester Towers* a unified novel? Does it matter if it is not?

(3) How seriously do you think Trollope takes the metaphor of 'war' between the groups of clergymen in Barchester?

(4) How purely comic a figure is Mrs Proudie *or* Mr Slope?

(5) How essential to the success of *Barchester Towers* is the effective management of plot?

(6) What significance does Trollope attach to place and setting in *Barchester Towers*?

(7) How much sympathy do you think Trollope means the reader to have for the signora?

(8) How significant is Trollope's narrator in influencing the reader's assessment of the action and the characters?

(9) 'Trollope's social comedy has an essentially conservative aim.' Do you agree?

(10) 'Trollope's sense of comedy does not depend on the circumstances of time and place; his characters are perennial types which can be found in any society at any time.' Do you agree?

Two specimen answers

(2) Is *Barchester Towers* a unified novel? Does it matter if it is not?

Barchester Towers is a novel in which complex strands of action are woven together. Some readers, however, may wonder whether they form a coherent pattern. It may be argued that it would not matter too much if they did not. Many novels are episodic. Their effect is cumulative; incident is heaped on incident, and each is enjoyed for its own sake. Some loose thread may hold them together – a journey, a quest, the story of a life – but the connecting links are less significant than the episodes they join together. *Barchester Towers*, for all its air of happy spontaneity , is not a novel of this kind. It does possess some features of the quest novel, but what is pursued is a knowledge of what is valuable, which is only known when it is enjoyed. Four strands of the action can be distinguished: Mr Slope pursues power and wealth, the first through his profession as a clergyman, the second through marriage. He fails, because in Barchester these purposes are suspect: the ethos of the place rejects them. Mrs Proudie seeks power over the bishop; she succeeds, but since the bishop's power is limited by other circumstances which arise in the course of the action, her victory is confined to little more than the sphere of domestic life. One of the circumstances is the fact that Mr Arabin becomes Dean of Barchester, another is the defeat of Mr Slope. As Dean of Barchester, Mr Arabin becomes leader of the Cathedral and head of a party of clergymen devoted to upholding the ancient traditions of the Church of England against reforming zeal. By marrying Eleanor Bold he joins a family which includes Archdeacon Grantly and Mr Harding, thus knitting together forces which respect old customs and established values, which Bishop Proudie's party appeared to threaten. The moral order of Barchester seemed also threatened by the amorality of the Stanhopes, but the signora acknowledges the superiority of the power of love, and the Stanhopes retire to Italy. It may seem difficult to include the Thornes and De Courcys and their tenants in this account. They represent a secular version of the same struggle for order. But the values of the Thornes, though supportive of all that is best in the traditions of the country, are not equal to the demands of changing times. Perhaps it is not without significance that Mr Thorne is a bachelor and Miss Thorne an old maid. The active future lies with the Arabins, but it is Mr Harding who has shown throughout the novel the reconciling power of love. Despite its complexity, *Barchester Towers* offers an aesthetically satisfying unity of theme.

(3) How essential to the success of *Barchester Towers* is the effective management of plot?

The notion of 'plot' is complex. By it we mean the overall design of the novel, the elaboration of its action, the relation of its episodes to one another, of commentary and summary to dramatised scene, the patterns of imagery which the author uses, the repetitions of motif which together establish a rhythm and pattern which are aesthetically pleasing and intellectually satisfying. The main spring of Trollope's plot is surprise: it is supported by the habitual tone of gentle irony on the part of the narrator who smiles as he sees things turning out differently from what his characters expect. There are specific repetitions which help to sustain our sense of the shape and spirit of the novel. One small example is Trollope's early reference to *The Jupiter* (*The Times*) in which (at the end of Chapter 1) the prediction of Dr Proudie's accession to the bishopric of Barchester is made.

In Chapter 43, however, subtitled (in part) 'Mr Slope is encouraged by the Press', Trollope inserts a long leader from the *Jupiter* praising Mr Slope and suggesting that his appointment 'would go far to raise the confidence of the public in the present administration of church patronage'. Trollope ironically reflects on the excited expectations of Mr Slope and in the event suggests that the *Jupiter*'s infallibility is suspect.

Another example of pattern within the novel is the placing of the two main public events – Mrs Proudie's reception (at which the impact of the signora on Barchester is first felt with the consequent undermining of Mrs Proudie's confidence in Mr Slope) and Miss Thorne's outdoor fête (where the complications of Eleanor Bold's marriage prospects begin to simplify). The first event opens up the possibilities of narrative complication, the second begins to reduce them.

The constant element of surprise in Trollope's plot, however, has nothing arbitrary about it. Events are surprising, but, with hindsight, just what we might have expected. People are surprised because they have access to a limited view. Mr Slope's clever management of things at Puddingdale has to be reversed when he realises the possible benefit to himself of doing Mr Harding a favour. His victory over Mrs Proudie in the matter of the Quiverfuls is annulled when he finds that it might cost him the support of the bishop for his own claim to the deanery of Barchester. Considered abstractly, the plot of *Barchester Towers* is a means of expressing one of its most significant themes: those who adhere to absolute morality are to be preferred to those who calculate the possible consequences of their actions. The latter can never be sure about outcomes; the former, if they are true to the ideals of goodness and of love, will make no irremediable mistakes.

Part 5

Suggestions for further reading

The text

There is no complete edition of all Trollope's novels. *Barchester Towers* has been edited by R.W. Chapman for the Oxford Trollope (Oxford University Press, Oxford, 1953). This edition with a new introduction by James R. Kincaid has been published as a World's Classics paperback by Oxford University Press, Oxford, 1980. Its text is divided into two volumes. The novel has also been edited with an introduction and notes by David Skilton, Pan Books, London, 1980. The best edition for the student is to be found in the Penguin English Library with an introduction and notes by Robin Gilmour, Penguin Books, Harmondsworth, 1983. The text follows the division into three volumes of the first edition, published in 1857 by Longman.

Other works by Trollope

Anthony Trollope wrote over forty novels. After his two early Irish novels, *The Macdermots of Ballycloran* (1847) and *The Kellys and the O'Kellys* (1848), he wrote six novels set in Barsetshire: *The Warden* (1855); *Barchester Towers* (1857); *Doctor Thorne* (1858); *Framley Parsonage* (1861); *The Small House at Allington* (1864); and *The Last Chronicle of Barset* (1867). Another group of novels which explores the world of politics consists of *Can You Forgive Her?* (1864); *Phineas Finn* (1869); *The Eustace Diamonds* (1873); *Phineas Redux* (1874); *The Prime Minister* (1876) and *The Duke's Children* (1880). Other novels include *Orley Farm* (1862); *The Belton Estate* (1866); *The Claverings* (1867); *He Knew He was Right* (1869); *The Way We Live Now* (1875); *Dr Wortle's School* (1881) and *Ayala's Angel* (1881). *His Autobiography* (1883), published posthumously, is one of the best Victorian autobiographies.

General reading

CHADWICK, OWEN: *The Victorian Church*, Part 1, A. &. C. Black, London, 1966.

COCKSHUT, A.O.J.: *Anthony Trollope: a critical study*, Collins, London, 1955.

MILLER, J. HILLIS: *The Form of Victorian Fiction*, University of Notre Dame Press, Notre Dame, Indiana, 1968.

KNOEPFLMACHER, U.C.: *Laughter and Despair: Readings in Ten Novels of the Victorian Period*, University of California Press, Berkeley, 1971.

apROBERTS, RUTH: *The Moral Trollope*, Ohio University Press, Athens, Ohio, 1971.

SADLEIR, MICHAEL: *Trollope: a commentary*, Constable, London, 1927.

SMALLEY, DONALD (ED.): *Anthony Trollope: The Critical Heritage*, Routledge & Kegan Paul, London, 1969.

The author of these notes

IAN MILLIGAN was educated at the University of Glasgow where he gained the degrees of MA and MED. After teaching in the Royal High School, Edinburgh, he became a lecturer in English at Moray House College of Education, Edinburgh. He now lectures in the Department of English Studies at the University of Stirling. He has published articles on education, on the teaching of literature and on nineteenth- and twentieth-century literature. He is the author of York Notes on Jane Austen's *Northanger Abbey*, Richard Hughes's *A High Wind in Jamaica* and L. P. Hartley's *The Shrimp and the Anemone*, and the York Handbook on *The English Novel*.

York Notes: list of titles

CHINUA ACHEBE
A Man of the People
Arrow of God
Things Fall Apart

EDWARD ALBEE
Who's Afraid of Virginia Woolf?

ELECHI AMADI
The Concubine

ANONYMOUS
Beowulf
Everyman

JOHN ARDEN
Serjeant Musgrave's Dance

AYI KWEI ARMAH
The Beautyful Ones Are Not Yet Born

W. H. AUDEN
Selected Poems

JANE AUSTEN
Emma
Mansfield Park
Northanger Abbey
Persuasion
Pride and Prejudice
Sense and Sensibility

HONORÉ DE BALZAC
Le Père Goriot

SAMUEL BECKETT
Waiting for Godot

SAUL BELLOW
Henderson, The Rain King

ARNOLD BENNETT
Anna of the Five Towns

WILLIAM BLAKE
Songs of Innocence, Songs of Experience

ROBERT BOLT
A Man For All Seasons

ANNE BRONTË
The Tenant of Wildfell Hall

CHARLOTTE BRONTË
Jane Eyre

EMILY BRONTË
Wuthering Heights

ROBERT BROWNING
Men and Women

JOHN BUCHAN
The Thirty-Nine Steps

JOHN BUNYAN
The Pilgrim's Progress

BYRON
Selected Poems

ALBERT CAMUS
L'Etranger (The Outsider)

GEOFFREY CHAUCER
Prologue to the Canterbury Tales
The Franklin's Tale
The Knight's Tale
The Merchant's Tale
The Miller's Tale
The Nun's Priest's Tale
The Pardoner's Tale
The Wife of Bath's Tale
Troilus and Criseyde

ANTON CHEKHOV
The Cherry Orchard

SAMUEL TAYLOR COLERIDGE
Selected Poems

WILKIE COLLINS
The Moonstone
The Woman in White

SIR ARTHUR CONAN DOYLE
The Hound of the Baskervilles

WILLIAM CONGREVE
The Way of the World

JOSEPH CONRAD
Heart of Darkness
Lord Jim
Nostromo
The Secret Agent
Victory
Youth and *Typhoon*

STEPHEN CRANE
The Red Badge of Courage

BRUCE DAWE
Selected Poems

WALTER DE LA MARE
Selected Poems

DANIEL DEFOE
A Journal of the Plague Year
Moll Flanders
Robinson Crusoe

CHARLES DICKENS
A Tale of Two Cities
Bleak House
David Copperfield
Great Expectations
Hard Times
Little Dorrit
Nicholas Nickleby
Oliver Twist
Our Mutual Friend
The Pickwick Papers

EMILY DICKINSON
Selected Poems

JOHN DONNE
Selected Poems

THEODORE DREISER
Sister Carrie

GEORGE ELIOT
Adam Bede
Middlemarch
Silas Marner
The Mill on the Floss

T. S. ELIOT
Four Quartets
Murder in the Cathedral
Selected Poems
The Cocktail Party
The Waste Land

J. G. FARRELL
The Siege of Krishnapur

GEORGE FARQUHAR
The Beaux Stratagem

WILLIAM FAULKNER
Absalom, Absalom!
As I Lay Dying
Go Down, Moses
The Sound and the Fury

HENRY FIELDING
Joseph Andrews
Tom Jones

F. SCOTT FITZGERALD
Tender is the Night
The Great Gatsby

E. M. FORSTER
A Passage to India
Howards End

ATHOL FUGARD
Selected Plays

JOHN GALSWORTHY
Strife

MRS GASKELL
North and South

WILLIAM GOLDING
Lord of the Flies
The Inheritors
The Spire

OLIVER GOLDSMITH
She Stoops to Conquer
The Vicar of Wakefield

ROBERT GRAVES
Goodbye to All That

GRAHAM GREENE
Brighton Rock
The Heart of the Matter
The Power and the Glory

THOMAS HARDY
Far from the Madding Crowd
Jude the Obscure
Selected Poems
Tess of the D'Urbervilles
The Mayor of Casterbridge
The Return of the Native
The Trumpet Major
The Woodlanders
Under the Greenwood Tree

L. P. HARTLEY
The Go-Between
The Shrimp and the Anemone

NATHANIEL HAWTHORNE
The Scarlet Letter

SEAMUS HEANEY
Selected Poems

ERNEST HEMINGWAY
A Farewell to Arms
For Whom the Bell Tolls
The African Stories
The Old Man and the Sea

GEORGE HERBERT
Selected Poems

HERMANN HESSE
Steppenwolf

BARRY HINES
Kes

HOMER
The Iliad

ANTHONY HOPE
The Prisoner of Zenda

GERARD MANLEY HOPKINS
Selected Poems

WILLIAM DEAN HOWELLS
The Rise of Silas Lapham

RICHARD HUGHES
A High Wind in Jamaica

THOMAS HUGHES
Tom Brown's Schooldays

ALDOUS HUXLEY
Brave New World

HENRIK IBSEN
A Doll's House
Ghosts
Hedda Gabler

HENRY JAMES
Daisy Miller
The Europeans
The Portrait of a Lady
The Turn of the Screw
Washington Square

SAMUEL JOHNSON
Rasselas

BEN JONSON
The Alchemist
Volpone

JAMES JOYCE
A Portrait of the Artist as a Young Man
Dubliners

JOHN KEATS
Selected Poems

RUDYARD KIPLING
Kim

D. H. LAWRENCE
Sons and Lovers
The Rainbow
Women in Love

CAMARA LAYE
L'Enfant Noir

HARPER LEE
To Kill a Mocking-Bird

LAURIE LEE
Cider with Rosie

THOMAS MANN
Tonio Kröger

CHRISTOPHER MARLOWE
Doctor Faustus
Edward II

ANDREW MARVELL
Selected Poems

W. SOMERSET MAUGHAM
Of Human Bondage
Selected Short Stories

J. MEADE FALKNER
Moonfleet

HERMAN MELVILLE
Billy Budd
Moby Dick

THOMAS MIDDLETON
Women Beware Women

THOMAS MIDDLETON *and* WILLIAM ROWLEY
The Changeling

ARTHUR MILLER
Death of a Salesman
The Crucible

JOHN MILTON
Paradise Lost I & II
Paradise Lost IV & IX
Selected Poems

V. S. NAIPAUL
A House for Mr Biswas

SEAN O'CASEY
Juno and the Paycock
The Shadow of a Gunman

GABRIEL OKARA
The Voice

EUGENE O'NEILL
Mourning Becomes Electra

GEORGE ORWELL
Animal Farm
Nineteen Eighty-four

JOHN OSBORNE
Look Back in Anger

WILFRED OWEN
Selected Poems

ALAN PATON
Cry, The Beloved Country

THOMAS LOVE PEACOCK
Nightmare Abbey and *Crotchet Castle*

HAROLD PINTER
The Birthday Party
The Caretaker

PLATO
The Republic

ALEXANDER POPE
Selected Poems

THOMAS PYNCHON
The Crying of Lot 49

SIR WALTER SCOTT
Ivanhoe
Quentin Durward
The Heart of Midlothian
Waverley

PETER SHAFFER
The Royal Hunt of the Sun

WILLIAM SHAKESPEARE
A Midsummer Night's Dream
Antony and Cleopatra
As You Like It
Coriolanus
Cymbeline
Hamlet
Henry IV Part I
Henry IV Part II
Henry V
Julius Caesar
King Lear
Love's Labour's Lost
Macbeth
Measure for Measure
Much Ado About Nothing
Othello
Richard II
Richard III
Romeo and Juliet
Sonnets
The Merchant of Venice
The Taming of the Shrew
The Tempest
The Winter's Tale
Troilus and Cressida
Twelfth Night
The Two Gentlemen of Verona

GEORGE BERNARD SHAW
Androcles and the Lion
Arms and the Man
Caesar and Cleopatra
Candida
Major Barbara
Pygmalion
Saint Joan
The Devil's Disciple

MARY SHELLEY
Frankenstein

PERCY BYSSHE SHELLEY
Selected Poems

RICHARD BRINSLEY SHERIDAN
The School for Scandal
The Rivals

WOLE SOYINKA
The Lion and the Jewel
The Road
Three Short Plays

EDMUND SPENSER
The Faerie Queene (Book I)

JOHN STEINBECK
Of Mice and Men
The Grapes of Wrath
The Pearl

LAURENCE STERNE
A Sentimental Journey
Tristram Shandy

ROBERT LOUIS STEVENSON
Kidnapped
Treasure Island
Dr Jekyll and Mr Hyde

TOM STOPPARD
Professional Foul
Rosencrantz and Guildenstern are Dead

JONATHAN SWIFT
Gulliver's Travels

JOHN MILLINGTON SYNGE
The Playboy of the Western World

TENNYSON
Selected Poems

W. M. THACKERAY
Vanity Fair

DYLAN THOMAS
Under Milk Wood

EDWARD THOMAS
Selected Poems

FLORA THOMPSON
Lark Rise to Candleford

J. R. R. TOLKIEN
The Hobbit
The Lord of the Rings

CYRIL TOURNEUR
The Revenger's Tragedy

ANTHONY TROLLOPE
Barchester Towers

MARK TWAIN
Huckleberry Finn
Tom Sawyer

VIRGIL
The Aeneid

VOLTAIRE
Candide

EVELYN WAUGH
Decline and Fall
A Handful of Dust

JOHN WEBSTER
The Duchess of Malfi
The White Devil

H. G. WELLS
The History of Mr Polly
The Invisible Man
The War of the Worlds

ARNOLD WESKER
Chips with Everything
Roots

PATRICK WHITE
Voss

OSCAR WILDE
The Importance of Being Earnest

TENNESSEE WILLIAMS
The Glass Menagerie

VIRGINIA WOOLF
To the Lighthouse

WILLIAM WORDSWORTH
Selected Poems

W. B. YEATS
Selected Poems